The New Gourmet

SENSATIONAL & SATISFYING LOW-FAT COOKING

MARY HARRISON CARROLL
Writer

HAL STRAUS
Editor

CALIFORNIA CULINARY ACADEMY

Mary Carroll has been teaching the principles and techniques of healthy cooking for many years. She is the founder of Cuisine Naturelle, the West Coast's first natural foods cooking school, and is a nationally known writer on healthy cuisine for such publications as *American Health* and *Medical Self-Care.* Her recipes and unique approach have been featured in *USA Today,* Time-Life Cookbooks, and many television programs. She is the author of the California Culinary Academy cookbook *Healthy Cooking: Fresh Gourmet Meals in Minutes* and a national syndicated cooking column, "Cuisine Naturelle" (formerly "Laurel's Kitchen"). As the cook for the Preventive Medicine Research Institute in San Francisco, she created the recipes used in a major study of the effects of diet on reversing heart disease. Mary currently resides in the Minneapolis area, where she teaches healthy-cooking classes and writes.

The California Culinary Academy In the forefront of American institutions leading the culinary renaissance in this country, the California Culinary Academy in San Francisco has gained a reputation as one of the most outstanding professional chef training schools in the world. With a teaching staff recruited from the best restaurants of Western Europe, the Academy educates students from around the globe in the preparation of classical cuisine. The recipes in this book were created in consultation with the chefs of the Academy. For information about the Academy, write the Office of the Dean, California Culinary Academy, 625 Polk Street, San Francisco, CA 94102.

Front Cover
Herbed saffron rice makes an elegant foundation for Basque Paella—the traditional Spanish one-pot dish of seafood, shellfish, chicken, and colorful vegetables (page 94).

Title Page
Orange peel, fennel, and thyme flavor this hearty, low-calorie fish soup from Southern France—Mary's Bourride (page 28).

Back Cover

Upper Fresh vegetables and lean chicken are featured in this quick, authentic, Oriental stir-fry entrée (page 85).

Lower A packet of cooking parchment yields its savory filling of Chicken Baked with Tomatoes and Herbs (page 79).

Special Thanks to Staff and students of Cuisine Naturelle; Dr. Dean Ornish; Jeffrey Long, Surface Studios, San Francisco, Calif.

Contributors

Photographer
Michael Lamotte

Food Stylist
Susan Devaty

Photographic Stylist
Sara Slavin

Calligraphers
Keith Carlson, Chuck Wertman

Consultant
Jane Rubey, M.P.H., R.D.

Additional Photographers
Laurie Black, Academy photography; Alan Copeland, Academy photography; Marshall Gordon, pages 119, 123; Beth Marsolais, author, at left; Bob Montesclaros, page 76; Kit Morris, chefs, at left; Jackson Vereen, page 93

Additional Stylists
Doug Warne, page 76; M. Susan Broussard, page 93

Photographer's Assistant
Bruce E. James

Assistant Food Stylist
Kathleen Lewis

Copyeditors
Andrea Y. Connolly, Judith Dunham

Proofreader
Karen K. Johnson

Designers
Linda Hinrichs
Carol Kramer

Printed in Hong Kong through Mandarin Offset.

The California Culinary Academy series is published by the staff of Cole Group.

Publisher
Brete C. Harrison

VP and Director of Operations
Linda Hauck

VP Marketing and Business Development
John A. Morris

Associate Publisher
James Connolly

Director of Production
Steve Lux

Senior Editor
Annette Gooch

Production Assistant
Dotti Hydue

Address all inquiries to
Cole Group
4415 Sonoma Highway/PO Box 4089
Santa Rosa, CA 95402-4089
(800) 959-2717   (707) 538-0492
FAX (707) 538-0497

Distributed to the book trade by Publishers Group West.

C O N T E N T S

Count calories, plan meals and make them ahead—and be sure to include a wide variety of tasty dishes.

The Gourmet Dieter

O nly a wide variety of flavorful, satisfying, low-calorie dishes will assure that you achieve your weight-control goals. In this chapter, you will discover the right ingredients and cooking techniques to use in preparing elegant, low-calorie cuisine. Easy-reference charts help you determine your specific weight-control goals and which foods to avoid and which foods to enjoy to stay healthy during the dieting process (see page 10). A special feature helps you plan for the "danger zones" of social occasions, restaurants, and travel dining (see page 11). Tips on shopping and organizing your kitchen for weight maintenance end the chapter—and start you on the road to elegant, low-calorie cooking.

THE GOURMET WAY TO LOWER WEIGHT

Contrary to popular belief, losing weight—or maintaining your current weight—does not have to be an ordeal of eating ordinary, bland foods and of experiencing relentless hunger. Using the right ingredients, recipes, and cooking techniques, you can prepare tasty, satisfying, sophisticated menus and accomplish your weight goals at the same time.

What's more, low-calorie cooking can be fun, easy, and quick, even if you are busy with a career, or a family, or both. In fact, the recipes in this book were selected not only for their low-calorie content and delicious flavors but also for their ease of preparation.

What exactly is elegant low-calorie cooking? First, it is cooking done with a gourmet touch. In planning and creating meals, a gourmet cook pays special attention to the latest culinary techniques, the superior quality of the ingredients, and the style of presentations. Gourmet cooking need not be a complex process. Simple steps and simple ingredients are fine; attention to detail is the key.

An uncomplicated salad, such as Jicama and Citrus Salad (see page 50), can be an elegant dish. The vegetables, which should be especially fresh, are tossed with slices of orange. Then a light oil and lemon juice dressing is added. Not much time, not many unusual ingredients, but you might pay quite a bit for this salad served in an upscale restaurant.

Once a dish is prepared, a gourmet enjoys its subtleties of taste, texture, and presentation. A gourmet appreciates food with the eye as well as the palate.

In addition to its focus on fine food, this book has another dimension: The recipes are all low in calories. They are based on techniques that allow you to prepare delicious cuisine and help control your weight at the same time, such as lowering the calories in Chinese stir-fry dishes by using a combination of wine and flavorful oils instead of 100 percent oil; marinating skinned poultry and lean beef before cooking to retain the moistness that is often lost in lower fat entrées; and reducing a poaching sauce for an elegant fruit dessert.

You'll find new ideas for innovative gourmet dishes, timesaving tips, and special notes on how the dishes can be cooked ahead and frozen for easy after-work meals. Also included are complete menus and numerous hints for easy, elegant entertaining.

To ensure optimum flavor, the recipes focus on fresh ingredients—fruits and vegetables; lean meats, poultry, and fish; and low-fat dairy products. Many of the recipes use sherry or wine (instead of oil or fat) for sautéing vegetables to create a "flavor seal" as the food cooks. Flavored vinegars, fresh herbs and spices, nonfat yogurt, low-calorie mayonnaise, safflower oil, part-skim cheeses, and other good-tasting, good-quality low-calorie foods and seasonings replace their fattening (and often unhealthy) counterparts. The net result is that your taste buds enjoy the treat and you control your weight at the same time.

About the Recipes

The recipes in this book are sophisticated and satisfying, but they are also designed with the busy person in mind; almost all require less than one hour to cook, and most a lot less than that. *Preparation times* (how long the average cook takes to prepare the ingredients) are given for each recipe, along with *Cooking, Chilling,* or *Marinating times,* as applicable.

The number of *Calories per serving* is provided for each recipe so you can plan a week of meals and menus. Portion size has been carefully calculated. You'll notice that the portions are substantial but not large—you don't need to eat a great deal to feel satisfied due to the abundant use of complex carbohydrates (see page 9).

Most of the recipes yield four to eight servings, but almost all can be halved without changing the proportions of the ingredients. You might also try making the full recipe and packaging the leftovers to serve at another time. All dishes, except the salads and some of the desserts, generally freeze beautifully.

If you're going to eat less, the recipes you prepare must be exciting and varied. The recipes in this book span the globe, featuring dishes from Greece, China, Japan, the Middle East, Thailand, and other exotic places. The variety of styles and cuisines will ensure your continued interest.

A Word of Caution

Please note that this book does not offer a strict weight-loss program. Nor does it promote any miraculous dietetic food that will bore you with its repetition and finally disappoint you with its lack of results. Effective, healthy dieting depends on using a wide variety of nutritious foods prepared for delicious dining—foods that are new and different enough to avoid the boredom of routine, yet easy to prepare. This way you can design your diet around your needs, and then stick to it.

Any large weight loss should be achieved over a period of several weeks or months. The body has a daily requirement of essential nutrients to maintain its chemical balance and state of health. If you attempt a crash diet, you will most likely lose water weight and possibly damage the body protein stores that maintain muscle and organ tissue. If you want to drop ten or more pounds, you should lose that weight healthfully, over a period of five to ten weeks. You'll probably keep the weight off longer and stay healthier.

To ensure your health during the dieting process, the recipes in this book emphasize nutrition, incorporating protein, complex carbohydrates, high fiber content, vitamins and minerals, low salt and sugar, and unprocessed foods. You should always consult your physician, however, before embarking on any new diet. If you have a current or previous health condition, you may have to take special precautions.

HOW YOU LOSE WEIGHT

There is nothing mysterious about losing weight or maintaining your current weight. Essentially, weight control results from three aspects of your daily life working harmoniously—diet, attitude, and exercise.

Diet

Calories are simply units of energy measurement. You take in a certain number of calories during the day and you burn off a like amount—that is, if your body is functioning well. Weight maintenance is like balancing a budget: If you earn more than you spend, you build up deposits; if you eat more calories than your body can use, you gain weight.

Body fat contains 3,500 calories per pound. Therefore, in order to lose one pound of weight, you must eat 3,500 fewer calories than your body can use.

For example, an overweight, moderately active man who wants to lose one pound can eat 500 calories less each day for seven days, and he will drop that pound in a week's time. If he eats 1,000 calories less each day for a week, he'll lose two pounds. Moderate activity, preferably exercise, helps him maintain his weight or shed the pounds more quickly.

To plan an effective weight-loss strategy, first you must calculate the amount of calories your body needs to maintain its normal energy level. A healthy adult at a moderate activity level requires about 15 calories per pound of body weight per day. Determine your ideal body weight by referring to the Desirable Weight Chart above. You will have to make a subjective judgment on your body frame to come up with an exact figure within the given range. Multiply this number by 15 to get your daily calorie requirement.

To lose weight, you will have to eat less than your daily calorie requirement. Here's an example: Judy exercises moderately but weighs about 135 pounds. She is 5' 4" and has a medium frame, so she calculates her ideal weight at about 125 pounds. She wants to lose 10 pounds.

DESIRABLE WEIGHT CHART

MEN*

HEIGHT (in 1-inch heels)	WEIGHT (in pounds)**		
	Small Frame	Medium Frame	Large Frame
5'2"	128–134	131–141	138–150
5'3"	130–136	133–143	140–153
5'4"	132–138	135–145	142–156
5'5"	134–140	137–148	144–160
5'6"	136–142	139–151	146–164
5'7"	138–145	142–154	149–168
5'8"	140–148	145–157	152–172
5'9"	142–151	148–160	155–176
5'10"	144–154	151–163	158–180
5'11"	146–157	154–166	161–184
6'0"	149–160	157–170	164–188
6'1"	152–164	160–174	168–192
6'2"	155–168	164–178	172–197
6'3"	158–172	167–182	176–202
6'4"	162–176	171–187	181–207

WOMEN*

HEIGHT (in 1-inch heels)	WEIGHT (in pounds)**		
	Small Frame	Medium Frame	Large Frame
4'10"	102–110	109–121	118–131
4'11"	103–113	111–123	120–134
5'0"	104–115	113–126	122–137
5'1"	106–118	115–129	125–140
5'2"	108–121	118–132	128–143
5'3"	111–124	121–135	131–147
5'4"	114–127	124–138	134–151
5'5"	117–130	127–141	137–155
5'6"	120–133	130–144	140–159
5'7"	123–136	133–147	143–163
5'8"	126–139	136–150	146–167
5'9"	129–142	139–153	149–170
5'10"	132–145	142–156	152–173
5'11"	135–148	145–159	155–176
6'0"	138–151	148–162	158–179

*According to body frame, ages 25–59
**In indoor clothing weighing 5 pounds for men and 3 pounds for women.

Source: Metropolitan Life Insurance Co., New York. Copyright 1983.

To figure her daily caloric needs, Judy multiplies 125 by 15, which equals 1,875. Subtracting 500 from this number gives her 1,375—the daily calorie count she will aim for while on her diet. In one week, assuming she gets the same amount of exercise, Judy will lose one pound. In 10 weeks, she'll lose 10 pounds: her goal.

The quantity of calories you consume each day can be regulated by the ingredients you use and the size of your servings. Start to think thin. Choose small portions, such as four ounces of meat or fish or a smaller than usual slice of bread. Eat more salad or steamed vegetables to offset the smaller portions of higher calorie items. Cook with low-calorie recipes, such as the ones in this book.

An important but often neglected aspect of weight management is the variety of foods consumed. Many people, bored with a repetitive diet, tend to eat more of the same food to compensate for the lack of variety. Of course, this doesn't help control weight. Eating a greater variety of foods will help you maintain your diet and reach your weight-control goals. Imaginative recipes, such as Pesto Summer Vegetable Soup (see page 35) and Eggplant and Chick-pea Moussaka (see page 56), prevent boredom, allowing you to prepare tasty meals for weeks at a time without increasing calories.

Attitude

The kinds of foods you eat are often related to emotional or psychological needs, not to true physical

CALORIE BURN-OFF CHART

Calories used per hour	Activities	
120–150	Strolling 1 mph Light housework	Walking 2 mph
150–240	Typing (manual) Riding lawn mower	Golf (using power cart)
240–300	Cleaning windows Mopping floors Vacuuming Pushing light power mower Bowling	Walking 3 mph Cycling 6 mph Golf (pulling cart) Horseback riding (sitting to trot)
300–360	Scrubbing floors Walking 3.5 mph Cycling 8 mph Table tennis Badminton Volleyball	Golf (carrying clubs) Tennis (doubles) Calisthenics (many) Ballet exercises Dancing (fox-trot)
360–420	Walking 4 mph Cycling 10 mph Ice-skating	Roller-skating Horseback riding (posting to trot)
420–480	Lawn-mowing (manual) Walking 5 mph Cycling 11 mph	Tennis (singles) Waterskiing Folk (square) dancing
480–600	Sawing hardwood Jogging 5 mph Cycling 12 mph Downhill skiing	Paddleball Horseback riding (galloping) Basketball Mountain climbing
600–660	Running 5.5 mph	Cycling 13 mph
Above 660	Running 6 or more mph Handball	Squash Ski touring (5 or more mph)

Source: "Physical Activity and Cardiovascular Health," *Modern Concepts of Cardiovascular Disease* 41 (1972): 25–30.

hunger. When you feel slightly dissatisfied with your workday, you might grab an ice cream at lunch or wolf down three pieces of bread and butter when you come home from work. Some recent studies have focused on so-called comfort foods, items people reach for when they are bored or unhappy. The foods may remind you of what your mother used to fix when you were sick or when she wanted to make you feel good.

You may be a victim of the "clean plate syndrome." Many people in their thirties and forties grew up in post-Depression households, where parents, burdened by the painful memories of leaner times, insisted that their children clean their plates before leaving the table. As the portion size grew over the years, the "clean plate syndrome" was too ingrained to be altered. Do you have difficulty leaving food on your plate—even when you're full? This habit can be leftover from childhood. Remember that you can usually save the food for another day, particularly recipes from this book.

Preparing meals that satisfy the eye as well as the palate can improve your attitude about eating. The feeling of accomplishment that comes from creating an especially satisfying—and nonfattening—meal can do a great deal for your attitude about yourself and your body.

Exercise

The rewards of regular exercise are both physical and psychological. When you exercise, you burn calories faster, which, of course, contributes to weight loss. The psychological benefits of exercising—a general feeling of well-being, relief from stress, enhanced self-image—work hand in hand with your weight-control goals.

The more strenuous the activity, the greater the consumption of calories. The Calorie Burn-off Chart above shows comparative calorie use of different activities, so that you can determine the most effective activities for your diet and exercise plan.

A NUTRITIONALLY SOUND APPROACH

As many dieters know, two weeks of eating celery sticks or dieter's milkshakes might take off the pounds, but it does not have a lasting effect. A sound nutritional program is an essential component of any worthwhile diet.

Certain foods and nutrients have proved indispensable for good health; others have been linked to disease and weight gain. Maybe you're already keeping an eye on cholesterol, fat, sodium, and sugar. If so, you'll be especially pleased by the recipes in this book because they do too.

FOODS TO AVOID

Although not a complete list, the following substances are either especially high in calories or have been associated with disease by scientific studies.

Fats

Low-calorie foods are generally low in fat. Fat has nine calories per gram; protein has less than half this amount. Therefore you can eat almost twice as much protein as fat without increasing the calories. Avoiding fatty foods will help your weight-loss or weight-maintenance program.

Some high-fat foods to avoid include high-fat dairy products such as high-fat cheeses, whole-milk products, and cream; nut butters; fatty meats and the skin on chicken; saturated fats that are solid at room temperature, including butter, margarine, and solid shortenings; mayonnaise; high-fat ice creams; calorie-laden cakes, cookies, and candies, which are also high in sugar.

Cholesterol

Found in the bloodstreams of most animals, cholesterol is a close companion to fats. Our bodies use cholesterol for many purposes but cannot always make use of the dietary cholesterol we consume in animal products such as meats, chicken, and dairy products. As a result, cholesterol can clog blood vessels and therefore has been linked to coronary disease.

For general health, you should avoid high-cholesterol foods, which are generally the same as fatty foods. Cholesterol is only found in animal products; it does not exist in vegetables, fruits, grains, and beans.

Sodium

Several studies have linked sodium with high blood pressure and heart attacks. You can reduce sodium intake by using low-sodium tamari or soy sauce instead of the regular version and trying some of the herbal salt substitutes that are available at supermarkets and health-food stores. If you have been salting everything for years, your taste buds may take about three months to revive. So be patient if you think some foods taste bland in the beginning.

Sugar

Although sugar accounts for one fifth of the average daily caloric intake, it provides almost no nutrients. It also places stress on the pancreas, the organ of the body that processes blood sugar, causing it to produce insulin in large quantities. This is not a problem for the healthy dieter, except that insulin also promotes fat storage. Therefore, every time you eat sugar, you add to your body fat. Candy contains many more calories per ounce than a piece of fresh fruit, and the sugar in it satisfies you less, often leading to uncontrolled eating.

Because sugar is such an abused substance in the average diet, it may take some effort to get "unhooked." If you're trying to shake a sweet tooth, stay away from artificially sweetened foods since they can also promote a craving for sugar. As you gradually wean yourself from sugar binges, substitute fresh fruit, juices, whole grains, and beans. These foods will fill you up and help balance your body's sugar-processing system.

VITAL NUTRIENTS

The following nutrients may not help take off the weight, but they will help you stay healthy during the weight-loss process.

Protein

Our culture has long depended on meat as its primary source of protein—over two thirds of our protein comes from animal sources. Meat is rich in protein, but it is higher in fat and cholesterol than vegetables, fruits, whole grains, and legumes. If you can get more of your protein from these complex carbohydrates, you reduce the amount of harmful saturated fats and cholesterol, while also cutting back on caloric intake. The recipes in this book concentrate on forms of protein with fewer calories, such as chicken and fish, as well as on complex carbohydrates.

Complex Carbohydrates

Before the invasion of refined flours and white bread, complex carbohydrates, or starches, were the main staples of many cultures. Found primarily in whole, unprocessed grains and legumes—lentils, kidney beans, split peas, brown rice, barley, corn, whole wheat, millet, and oats, among

The three elements of successful weight maintenance are preparing enticing low-calorie dishes, such as this Summer Melon Soup With Lime (see page 36), having an enjoyable exercise program, and maintaining a positive attitude about weight-control objectives.

WINNERS AND LOSERS

Use this chart for quick and easy reference on which foods to enjoy and which foods to avoid on your low-calorie eating plan.

Winners: Foods to Enjoy

The following "winners" were chosen for their above-average nutrient level, low calorie count, and excellent flavor—all important contributions to delicious low-calorie meals.

- ☐ Beans, such as lentils, split peas, kidney beans, black beans, and navy beans

- ☐ Chicken with skin removed

- ☐ Dark green leafy vegetables, such as spinach, chard, kale

- ☐ Fresh and dried herbs and spices

- ☐ Fresh fish and shellfish

- ☐ Fresh fruits, such as oranges, apples, pears, grapes, berries, peaches, grapefruit, and melon

- ☐ Fresh vegetables, such as carrots, celery, cucumber, radishes, broccoli, sprouts, green onions, zucchini, tomatoes, green beans, peas, corn, potatoes

- ☐ Fruit juices

- ☐ Herbal salt substitutes

- ☐ Herbal teas and grain-beverage coffee substitutes

- ☐ Oat bran and wheat bran

- ☐ Part skim cheeses, such as mozzarella, ricotta, and farmer cheese

- ☐ Safflower oil and olive oil in small quantities

- ☐ Whole grain breads and crackers

- ☐ Whole grains, such as brown rice, barley, oats, millet, whole wheat, and corn

Losers: Foods to Avoid

The foods in the following "losers" category provide few or no nutrients, add hefty calories in the form of fats, or may be detrimental to health.

- ☐ Avocado (in large quantity)

- ☐ Baked goods made with white flour and sugar

- ☐ Butter and margarine

- ☐ Chicken skin

- ☐ Cold cuts

- ☐ Deep-fried foods

- ☐ High-fat cheeses

- ☐ Hydrogenated oils and fats, such as hydrogenated nut butters, solid shortening

- ☐ Mayonnaise (except small quantities of low-calorie mayonnaise)

- ☐ Olives (in large quantity)

- ☐ Peanut butter

- ☐ Pork products, such as ham, bacon, scrapple

- ☐ Processed foods

- ☐ Salad dressings (most commercial dressings)

- ☐ Sardines

- ☐ Saturated fats, such as lard, coconut and palm oil

- ☐ Shortenings

- ☐ Sugar, brown sugar, and confectioners' sugar

others—complex carbohydrates contribute a great deal to health. They take longer to break down than other foods and help keep your body warm and your metabolism balanced by generating fuel that maintains consistent energy levels. Complex carbohydrates also help stave off the cravings for sugary cookies and the "empty calories" of other simple carbohydrates.

Simple carbohydrates are found primarily in sugars and refined starches such as white flour. Complex carbohydrates contain fiber, bran, germ, and other nutrients that are missing from sugar and refined starches. These nutrients are important in carbohydrate digestion since they allow the body to burn the carbohydrate for fuel at an even pace, providing energy as it is needed. We may get a burst of energy when we consume a simple carbohydrate, but often feel tired afterward as the system struggles to restore its nutrient levels.

Many weight-loss programs recommend including 40 percent or more complex carbohydrates in your diet. They are a good source of protein, are extremely low in fat and calories, and have plenty of fiber, vitamins, and minerals. If you have been following a lifelong diet of meat, high-fat dairy products, and canned or frozen vegetables, switching to complex carbohydrates might be difficult at first. Make the transition gradually by incorporating some beans into soups or salads, switching to a whole grain bread, or experimenting with some of the vegetarian entrées in this book, such as Barley-Stuffed Cabbage Rolls With Ginger Sauce (see page 54), or Bean Burgers (see page 65).

Fiber

Although fiber is not really a nutrient, it has been the focus of many nutritional studies. Fiber is a plant material that passes through the system without being digested, promoting the feeling of being pleasantly full and at the same time aiding elimination. Thus it is essential to a weight-loss program because it helps keep the colon and small intestines functioning well. Fiber is found in substantial amounts in whole, natural, unprocessed foods such as raw fruits and vegetables, granola cereal, brown rice, and whole grain breads. There is little, if any, fiber in animal products.

Vitamins and Minerals

Eating the vitamins and minerals essential for any diet involves knowing the cooking techniques that retain the optimum amount of vitamins and minerals in food, as well as using high-quality ingredients that are rich in these important nutrients. Fresh fruits and vegetables are among the best sources. Health-care professionals often recommend eating citrus fruits, a large green salad, or a steamed green vegetable in at least one meal each day to supply some of these essential nutrients. Switching from white flour products to whole grains also increases the level of vitamins and minerals in the diet.

Many nutritionists believe that vitamin and mineral supplements are important because the soil has been depleted of most of the necessary minerals, and fresh produce loses vitamins in the packing, shipping, and storing processes.

The importance of one mineral, calcium, has been known for several years, but research shows that most people don't get enough. Calcium is essential to bone strength and muscle function (it helps major muscles such as the heart contract and relax). Low-calorie, calcium-rich foods include the green leafy vegetables (you might try Audrey's Spinach Salad, page 42), some low-fat and nonfat milk products, whole grains, and beans.

Water

Most medical experts agree that drinking large amounts of water is an important health factor. Eight glasses a day, when you're moderately active or exercising and losing bodily fluids regularly, is generally recommended. Most experts, however, suggest drinking only a small amount of fluid at mealtime to ensure proper digestion.

LOW-CALORIE COOKING TECHNIQUES

It is not only what you eat but how you prepare it that will determine the success of your diet. Because certain techniques use less fat or bring out the rich flavor of seasonings, they are particularly appropriate for low-calorie meals.

Steaming and Poaching

When foods are steamed, they lose fewer nutrients than they do when boiled and, unless steamed too long, they retain more of their color. Try different steamers for different foods: the folding stainless steel steamer is good for chopped vegetables; stacking bamboo baskets are designed to hold larger vegetables and whole fish (see Steamed Fish With Ginger, page 92); the stainless steel colander steamer that fits into a pot is excellent for artichokes and large vegetables.

Poaching is similar to steaming, except that the food sits directly in the poaching liquid and absorbs its flavor. Favorite poaching liquids include broth, wine, sherry, and fruit juice. In this book, poaching is recommended for certain fish recipes (for example, Coquilles Sauce Verte, page 90) and for fruit desserts (Wine-Basted Pears, page 115) where the poaching wine is a main ingredient.

Baking and Roasting

An oven temperature of 350° F is called for in most of the baked recipes in this book, with the exception of the pastries, which require a slightly higher temperature. Make sure the baking pan contains enough liquid (the amount is usually specified in the recipe) so that the baked dish doesn't dry out while it cooks. These low-calorie recipes use low-salt stocks, juices, or wines (see Simple Baked Chicken With Orange and Cumin, page 77) to retain the moisture, rather than traditional, high-fat bases such as cream.

DANGER ZONES

Certain occasions are natural traps for the dieter. Just as you should learn about unknown terrain prior to a camping trip and then prepare accordingly, you should plan for special social occasions, dining in restaurants, and traveling.

Social Occasions Eating is a gregarious activity, connected with many social rituals such as Thanksgiving and Christmas dinners, weddings, and bar mitzvahs. You can avoid many potential danger zones by eating light at social occasions. Look for the fresh vegetable platter on the hors d'oeuvre table; eat a small meal before you leave home to prevent impulse eating; and ask for a dinner salad with dressing on the side or with fresh lemon or vinegar.

Restaurants Call ahead to see what low-calorie options the restaurant has on its menu. Learn to recognize low-calorie menu items, such as salads, lean meats and broiled fish, baked potatoes without sour cream (ask for plain yogurt), and fruit desserts.

This book has a special bonus for the frequent restaurant-goer—a wide assortment of international dishes you can prepare at home. With these gourmet recipes, you won't go out to eat as often and your weight-control plan will be much easier and much less expensive to follow.

Travel Plan ahead for travel: Call the airline 24 hours before flight time to request a special low-calorie meal; take along snack foods such as fruits, rice cakes, and fresh vegetable sticks; pack a few items—such as a low-calorie salad dressing, sweetener, or salt substitute—in a carry-on bag.

Booking a hotel room with a kitchenette or at least a refrigerator can save you a few restaurant meals. Stock it with low-calorie foods for quick breakfasts, lunches, and snacks.

Appropriate cookware enables you to use the most efficient low-calorie cooking techniques and makes low-calorie cooking more enjoyable. Invest in the essentials: a wok, a variety of steamers, an assortment of sharp knives, stainless steel pots, and a good blender or food processor.

Baking is a good way to avoid the high-calorie cooking methods of frying and deep-frying. Chicken and fish, for instance, are easily baked instead of fried and, if covered with a light sauce or salsa (see Mexican Baked Fish in Salsa Verde, page 91), will stay fresh and moist throughout the baking process.

Roasting preserves the tenderness of meats and vegetables. Slow roasting is usually done in a 300° F oven, and regular roasting in a 375° to 400° F oven. Roasted chicken and meats tend to emerge from the oven with a crisp skin and juicy interior. For chicken, where the skin is usually removed, the recipes in this book often suggest marinating or basting chicken before roasting to retain the juicy flavor (see Grilled Chicken in Sweet Marinade, page 75).

Broiling and Grilling

A boon to the busy cook, broiling is easy and quick. The low-calorie recipes featured in this book recommend broiling chicken and meat for the wonderfully rich flavors that develop during cooking. Broiled meats tend to retain their juices a little better than baked meats because they cook for less time and at a higher temperature. As with roasting, marinating or basting is often recommended.

Grilling has become a very popular way to prepare low-calorie entrées. Chicken, fish, and lean meats can be marinated before grilling to improve flavor. Cook all fish and the thinner cuts of meat and chicken right on the grill or in a stovetop grilling pan. Thicker sections or whole chickens need to be wrapped in aluminum foil and baked for 20 to 30 minutes before grilling in order to cook thoroughly. Grill small new potatoes right in their skins; corn on the cob can be grilled still wrapped in the husk. Other vegetables can be packaged in foil, sprinkled with water, lemon juice, or dry sherry, and steamed on the grill while the meat is cooking.

Sautéing and Stir-frying

Sauté derives from the French word for *leap* or *jump*, which is what properly sautéed food tends to do in an open skillet. A small amount of oil keeps vegetables, chicken, lean meat, and fish from sticking to the pan as they cook and seals in the moisture, ensuring that the food retains flavor and color.

Sautéing does not require a lot of oil. Small amounts of wine, sherry, stock, or water will serve the same purpose and will save calories. In the process of cooking, the alcohol in the wine evaporates, leaving the flavor without the calories. You can also use a small amount of oil for flavor (1 teaspoon per 6 cups of vegetables or meats). Add water if the sautéing food dries out during cooking. This process, actually called steam-sautéing, is similar to stir-frying.

Stir-frying is a type of sautéing that is done over very high heat. When stir-frying, you should stir the food constantly to prevent sticking. A wok is often used for stir-frying because its rounded bowl distributes heat evenly to the food. See page 79 for more tips on stir-frying.

COOKWARE FOR THE GOURMET DIETER

Gourmet low-calorie cooking does not require a great deal of expensive equipment. Choose durable cookware. Heavy-weight pots and pans are best for slow-cooking: soups, stews, grains and beans. Lighter pans are best for quick cooking: sautéing and stir-frying. Stainless steel or enamel-coated cast iron are now considered best for long-lasting cookware; in addition, some recent studies have linked Alzheimer's disease with consumption of excess aluminum, some of which might come from aluminum pots and pans.

You'll also want steamers (see page 11), a roasting pan with a rack, and perhaps a wok (see page 79). You may want to get a grill or a stovetop ridged grilling pan. A stainless steel pressure cooker is convenient for cooking beans in a hurry. Many of the recipes call for fresh lemon juice, so a juicer and strainer are handy items. You may also want to stock up on a few tin tart pans and ceramic soufflé dishes.

Always have three good knives on hand: one paring knife, one serrated knife, and one chopping knife, such as a 6- or 8-inch cook's knife. Keep them sharp with your own sharpener or have them sharpened professionally every six months or so. (A sharp knife actually causes fewer kitchen accidents than a dull one because it has less tendency to slip.) Keep knives on a magnetized knife rack or in a knife block, where they won't rub edges or become dull or knicked. Knives piled in a cutlery drawer can be very dangerous.

For maximum fat-free eating, a perforated spoon is helpful for lifting foods out of marinating and cooking liquids. A broad wok spatula makes stir-frying with a wok easier.

If you like your kitchen and your cookware, you'll enjoy cooking more, you'll eat out less (see Danger Zones, page 11), and losing weight will be that much easier.

Tips

... ON LOW-CALORIE EATING

Facing a full refrigerator on an empty stomach can be a challenge for any dieter. That's why you want to make preparations for those unexpected hungry moments.

☐ Know when your next meal is coming and take pleasure in the anticipation. Ask yourself why you feel like snacking. Is it because you are bored? Under stress? Do you need a transition from the work environment to the home environment? One researcher realized that all she needed was a transitional activity. After taking a shower or exercising the moment she came home from work, she lost the urge to raid the fridge.

☐ Always have some low-calorie snacks on hand. Scan "Hors d'Oeuvres and Appetizers" (see pages 15-25), where you will find finger foods that can serve as low-calorie transition foods to carry you until dinner.

☐ Keep a food diary. A week's entries will tell you how much those small snacks or extra touches—such as butter on steamed vegetables or catsup on a hamburger—are contributing to your weight problem. Buy a calorie-counter, available in many bookstores and supermarkets, and spend an hour analyzing it. You'll be amazed to learn the calories hidden in some foods.

☐ Read the labels on food packaging. The government requires that ingredients be listed in the order of their quantity in the product. If, for example, "corn syrup" is at the top of the ingredient list of a Japanese cooking wine, you'll do well to skip it. Simple sugars are inexpensive but the cost is high in fat and calories. If you choose to buy mirin or sake to prepare Asian stir-fry dishes, look for one of the many sugar-free brands that contain a simple list of familiar ingredients. Health-food stores often carry these brands.

☐ Organize the kitchen for weight maintenance. Go through cupboards, shelves, pantry, and refrigerator. Put all the packaged foods you won't be eating into a large cardboard box and give them away. Box cookware that you haven't used in years, keeping only the best pots and pans.

☐ Shop efficiently. Organize the shopping list into categories, such as produce, bulk foods, pantry, meats, and dairy. One theory holds that you can shop in a supermarket without entering the inner aisles and buy everything you need, since the perimeter holds all the fresh foods and the middle contains mostly processed foods and impulse items.

☐ Make meals ahead. When you plan ahead, you can cook elegant and imaginative meals. Preparing tested and nutritious low-calorie dishes from this book in advance is far better than improvising at the last moment and ending up with a caloric meal—or even worse, eating out. Many of the recipes in this book include directions on how to prepare a meal the night (or days) before; you may want to flag these recipes with a bookmark or marking pen for planning menus.

☐ Focus on enjoying the meal. Eating hurriedly can easily lead to being overweight. When you rush through a meal, your body regards it as an unpleasant activity, and what you eat matters less and less. It takes time and effort to learn to enjoy eating: Pay attention to how you prepare a meal, take time to relax before and during the meal, and give yourself the time to enjoy it.

Elegant low-calorie appetizers frequently utilize fresh garden vegetables and whole grain breads and crackers.

Hors d'Oeuvres & Appetizers

Appetizers and hors d'oeuvres are not usually considered appropriate for a low-calorie diet, but these recipes fit right in. They lend an elegant, international flair to a small dinner party or an hors d'oeuvre buffet and solve the dilemma of what to serve health-conscious guests when you entertain. In the party spirit, a special feature explains how to prepare appetizer platters for entertaining (see page 19), and a complete menu is presented for a holiday season hors d'oeuvre party (see page 24). The chapter also includes tips on creating delicious, low-calorie versions of your favorite dips (see page 23).

INTERNATIONAL APPETIZERS

These exotic, yet low-calorie recipes are especially suited for entertaining. Transport guests to foreign ports by creating a theme buffet around the various countries represented by the hors d'oeuvres. You might even identify each platter with a national flag or adorn it with other colorful decorations.

PITA QUESADILLAS

A favorite Mexican appetizer, these quesadillas (pronounced kay-suh-DEE-yuhs) are easy to make and use whole wheat pita bread, often lower in calories than regular breads, for the base. Wear rubber gloves to peel and seed the fresh chiles (the chile acids can sting sensitive skin).

- ½ cup grated part-skim mozzarella or low-fat Monterey jack cheese
- 3 small jalapeño chiles, seeded and diced
- 2 tablespoons chopped cilantro
- ¼ teaspoon ground cumin
- 2 tablespoons pimiento, drained and diced
- 2 large whole wheat pita breads

1. In a small bowl combine grated cheese, diced chile, cilantro, cumin, and pimiento.

2. With a sharp knife slice open pita breads along edges, making 4 thin rounds of bread. Lay, cut side up, on a parchment-covered baking sheet and sprinkle with cheese mixture.

3. Broil until bubbly. Cut each pita into 4 wedges. Serve hot.

Makes 16 wedges, 4 servings.

> *Calories per serving: 124*
> *Preparation time: 20 minutes*
> *Cooking time: 5 minutes*

ITALIAN ZUCCHINI PIZZAS

These "kid-sized" pizzas with a vegetable base are very easy for children to make and are great as snacks for adult weight watchers. The pizzas may be served as is or on thin low-calorie crackers.

- 2 thick zucchini (see Note)
- 1 cup Mary's Chunky Tomato Sauce With Fresh Basil (see page 109)
- ½ cup thinly sliced large mushrooms
- ¼ cup grated Parmesan or Romano cheese

1. Preheat oven to 200° F. Cut zucchini into round slices about ⅛ inch thick. Place on a parchment-lined baking sheet and bake until soft and moist but not brown (about 20 minutes).

2. Place 1 teaspoon sauce in center of each round, and then top with 1 slice mushroom and ½ teaspoon grated cheese.

3. Broil pizzas until lightly browned and bubbly. Serve hot.

Makes 20 small pizzas, 4 servings.

Note Rounds of eggplant may be substituted for zucchini.

> *Calories per serving: 23 per pizza*
> *Preparation time: 15 minutes*
> *Cooking time: 5 minutes*

MARINATED MUSHROOM AND CHICK-PEA APPETIZER

This tasty first course can also be served as a finger food along with other marinated vegetables. In Italian cookery, an antipasto can consist of any colorful vegetable, cooked or raw, and is usually presented before the pasta course. Serve your antipasto with crusty French bread.

- 2 cups button mushrooms, whole
- 2 cups chick-peas, cooked and drained
- 2 tablespoons capers
- 2 tablespoons minced parsley
- 2 tablespoons minced red onion
- 2 tablespoons white wine vinegar
- ⅓ cup olive oil
- 1 garlic clove, minced
- 1 teaspoon Dijon mustard
- ½ teaspoon honey
  Freshly ground pepper, to taste

1. Place mushrooms in one bowl and chick-peas and capers in another. Combine parsley, red onion, vinegar, and half of the oil; pour over chick-peas and capers. Mix remaining oil, garlic, mustard, honey, and pepper; pour over mushrooms.

2. Let both mixtures marinate for 6 to 8 hours.

3. Arrange a small serving of each on a leaf of lettuce or spinach. Mix remaining marinades together and spoon over chick-pea antipasto.

Serves 4.

> *Calories per serving: 309*
> *Preparation time: 15 minutes*
> *Marinating time: 6-8 hours*

STUFFED CHILES

A favorite from the American Southwest, this recipe calls for fresh chiles; if they are unavailable in your area, use canned chiles or pimientos instead. Use a small paring knife to slit chiles and remove seeds and membrane. These chiles are great served with a mug of sangria and a platter of low-calorie, unsalted tortilla chips.

12 fresh Anaheim chiles (also known as California chiles)
1 teaspoon safflower oil, for baking dish
¼ cup dry sherry
1 teaspoon olive oil
½ cup minced yellow onion
½ cup minced mushroom caps
1 bunch spinach, washed, stemmed, and chopped
½ cup grated part-skim mozzarella cheese
1 cup farmer cheese
2 cups rye bread crumbs, coarsely ground
½ teaspoon ground cumin
¼ teaspoon cayenne pepper
Salt or herbal salt substitute, to taste

1. Preheat oven to 400° F. Leaving stems on chiles, slit lengthwise and remove seeds and white membrane (see Note). Set, cut side up, in lightly oiled baking dish.

2. In a medium skillet heat sherry and olive oil until mixture is simmering. Stir in onion and cook over medium-high heat. Keep stirring until onion begins to brown slightly. Add mushrooms and cover; lower heat and cook until mushrooms weep moisture. (Add small amount of water if necessary to prevent mushrooms from sticking.) Remove cover and add spinach. Cover again and cook until wilted (about 3 minutes).

3. Remove from heat and add cheeses, bread crumbs, cumin, cayenne, and salt; mix well. Stuff chiles with mushroom mixture.

4. Bake until chiles are softened and cheeses have melted (about 30 minutes). Serve hot.

Makes 12 chiles, 6 servings.

<u>Note</u> When you are cutting chiles, it is a good safety precaution to wear rubber gloves. The chiles' pungent oils can sting fingers and then be transferred to eyes. Gloves also protect fingers from the sharp blade of the paring knife.

Calories per serving: 160
Preparation time: 45 minutes
Cooking time: 30 minutes

Mild Anaheim chiles are baked and stuffed with a savory sauté of diced mushroom, onion, spinach, and cheese. For a tasty prelude to a southwestern dinner, serve Stuffed Chiles with a mug of sangria.

ARMENIAN MEATBALLS

This recipe gets its Armenian flavor from the cumin. The meatballs are easy to make ahead and will freeze well. This tasty hors d'oeuvre can be served in an elegant fondue pot set over a hot plate or candle warmer. Provide guests with fondue forks or toothpicks.

- 2 slices whole wheat bread
- 1 pound extralean ground beef or lamb
- 1 clove garlic, minced
- 1 teaspoon ground cumin Black pepper, to taste
- 1½ cup peeled and chopped plum tomatoes
- ¾ cup low-calorie tomato sauce

1. Preheat oven to 350° F. Soften bread in tap water and then squeeze out excess liquid (to make the bread absorb more flavor than if used dry). In a large mixing bowl, mash together bread, beef, garlic, and cumin. Add black pepper, if desired.

2. Form into 2-inch-diameter meatballs and place in lightly oiled or nonstick skillet over medium heat.

3. Fry lightly on all sides until brown, pouring off any fat that develops. Transfer meatballs to an electric slow cooker or baking dish.

4. Blend tomatoes and tomato sauce and pour over meatballs. Bake for 1 hour (or cook in an electric slow cooker over high heat for 2 hours). Serve hot with the sauce.

Makes 24 to 30 meatballs, 6 servings.

Calories per serving: 200-250
Preparation time: 45 minutes
Cooking time: 1 hour

SUNOMONO

A delicious Japanese salad, often served in gourmet sushi bars, sunomono is traditionally a combination of grated or thinly sliced vegetables that have been marinated in a lemon-vinegar sauce. It is served before tempura or other fried foods to freshen the palate. Serve in lettuce cups or in small, shallow bowls. This dish makes a light and refreshing first course for a stir-fry dinner.

- 1 cup shrimp meat
- 7 tablespoons rice vinegar
- 1 tablespoon lemon juice
- 1 tablespoon dark sesame oil
- 5 tablespoons honey Pinch of salt or herbal salt substitute (see Note)
- 1½ large cucumbers, peeled, seeded, and coarsely grated
- 2 green onions, minced
- ¼ cup finely shredded green cabbage

Mix all ingredients in a bowl and let marinate 2 hours before serving. Serve slightly chilled.

Serves 4 as light first course or 8 as hors d'oeuvres.

Note Several research studies have linked sodium to high blood pressure and heart disease. To keep your sodium count down, this recipe (and many others throughout this book) recommends herbal salt substitutes, available in most supermarkets and health-food stores.

Calories per serving: 182
Preparation time: 15 minutes
Marinating time: 2 hours

PARTY PLEASERS

Here are several favorites for parties. They will become regulars in your entertaining repertoire because of their easy preparation, low number of calories, and winning flavors. The Cherry Tomatoes Stuffed With Ricotta (see page 20) is particularly tasty and low in calories.

MUSTARD CHICKEN WINGS

These chicken wings are brushed with a sweet and spicy mixture of cayenne pepper, mustard, garlic, and date sugar (ground, dried dates), and are baked to a crunch.

- 12 chicken wings Freshly ground black pepper, to taste
- 1 tablespoon date sugar or honey Cayenne pepper, to taste
- 1 clove garlic, finely minced
- 2 teaspoons Dijon mustard Whole wheat bread crumbs, very finely ground Oil, for greasing baking sheet

1. Preheat oven to 400° F. Remove as much skin as possible from wings. Sprinkle chicken with black pepper.

2. Combine date sugar, cayenne, garlic, and mustard. Brush mixture onto chicken, coating both sides lightly and evenly. Then dip chicken in bread crumbs.

3. Place on a lightly greased baking sheet and bake until light brown (about 30 minutes). Serve hot.

Serves 4.

Calories per serving: 395
Preparation time: 20 minutes
Baking time: 30 minutes

PREPARING HORS D'OEUVRES FOR ENTERTAINING

When planning your selection of appetizers for a party, consider the following.

Serving temperature Try to offer variety—a few hot hors d'oeuvres, a few at room temperature, and one or two chilled.

Shape Vary the shapes, arranging both round shapes and long, thin shapes on the same platter. For example, offer a scooped-out red bell pepper, filled with a low-calorie cheese dip, accompanied by round melba toasts and raw vegetable sticks.

Color Serve an assortment of warm colors—red, orange, yellow (tomatoes, oranges, and squash)—and cool colors—green, purple, blue (lettuce, eggplant, blueberries)—for alluring hors d'oeuvre combinations. The contrasts are especially effective when combined on the same platter.

Texture Choose crunchy- and smooth-textured foods. For example, serve a creamy dip with a crisp spear of Belgian endive or a crunchy slice of bell pepper. Strive for good texture throughout the setting as well. Use woven baskets, polished brass or copper trays, rattan mats, or bright cotton cloths as backgrounds for the food.

Preparing Vegetables for A Crudités Platter

Many vegetables can be transformed into wonderful dip containers or stuffed for appetizers. Small pumpkins, eggplant, bell peppers, or large, ripe tomatoes can be hollowed out to hold dips for a crudités platter. Smaller vegetables can be scooped out with a melon baller, stuffed with a cheese mixture or a vegetable pâté, and served as finger food.

To prepare a crudités platter, you can line the serving dish with lettuce that has been washed and checked for brown spots. Good vegetables for crudités platters include cherry tomatoes, celery and carrot sticks, broccoli and cauliflower florets, red or green bell pepper strips, whole banana peppers or small sweet chiles, green onions, whole snow peas or pea pods, diagonal slices of yellow summer squash, whole button mushrooms, endive spears, and asparagus tips. You may want to heat a small pot of water to boiling, and blanch the hard vegetables—broccoli, squash, peppers, carrots, and cauliflower.

When arranging the prepared vegetables on the platter, try to create interest by placing different colors and shapes together. For example, a long, green asparagus stalk might be placed next to a round, red cherry tomato for a colorful effect.

CHERRY TOMATOES STUFFED WITH RICOTTA

This recipe has become a popular one at California parties and weddings where health is a priority. The stuffed tomatoes are beautiful to serve, and, in small quantity, are easy to make. When buying cherry tomatoes, look for fully ripened, red tomatoes if you are planning to make this recipe immediately, or green ones if you are planning to make it later. Tomatoes will ripen quickly at room temperature. After ripening, tomatoes should be kept at 50° F or lower.

You can prepare the filling and hollow out the cherry tomatoes ahead of time (and keep them wrapped in plastic in the refrigerator), but stuff them just before serving. Once filled with the cheese mixture, they lose their freshness within a few hours.

    24 cherry tomatoes
    ⅓ cup part-skim ricotta cheese
    2 tablespoons finely grated
       Parmesan cheese
    2 tablespoons minced parsley
    1 tablespoon minced garlic

1. With a sharp knife, cut off the stem and a "cap" from each cherry tomato and reserve. Using the small end of a melon baller, scoop out the pulp from the tomato. Save pulp for another use.

2. In a small bowl, combine cheeses, parsley, and garlic. Spoon some of the mixture, approximately 1 to 2 teaspoons, into each tomato. Place cap on top. Serve slightly chilled on a bed of greens.

*Makes 24 cherry tomatoes,
6 servings.*

*Calories per serving: 44
Preparation time: 30 minutes*

STUFFED BROILED MUSHROOMS

Large white-capped mushrooms work best for this recipe. Choose mushrooms with stems that are slightly pulled away from the undersides of the caps; they will be easier to stem and stuff. This appetizer can be frozen before final broiling, if desired.

    12 large mushrooms
    1 teaspoon safflower oil
    1 small onion, finely chopped
    1 cup whole wheat bread
       crumbs, finely ground
    ¼ cup minced almonds
    1 tablespoon sherry
    ¼ teaspoon marjoram
       Freshly ground black pepper,
       to taste (optional)

1. Preheat broiler. Remove stems from mushrooms by wiggling at base (stems should pop out). Chop stems finely and set aside.

2. Place caps with open side down on baking sheet and broil for 2 minutes or until caps become wrinkled and begin to weep moisture. Let cool. Keep broiler hot.

3. Heat oil in skillet and sauté onion until soft, then add the chopped mushroom stems. Cook until mushrooms begin to weep moisture (about 8 minutes). Add bread crumbs, almonds, sherry, marjoram, and pepper, if desired, and cook 1 minute longer.

4. Stuff bread crumb filling into mushroom caps and place filled side up on baking sheet. Broil until light brown. Serve hot.

*Makes 12 stuffed mushrooms,
4 servings.*

*Calories per serving: 135
Preparation time: 20 minutes
Baking time: 5 minutes*

SAVORY NUT BALLS

Made with a combination of ground nuts and seeds, these savory little appetizers are about as low-calorie as you can find. They can be made ahead and frozen, so they are a great party hors d'oeuvre.

    ¾ cup walnuts, finely ground
    ½ cup sunflower seeds, finely
       ground
    ½ cup cashews, finely ground
    ¼ cup almonds, finely ground
    1 small onion, coarsely grated
    2 eggs, beaten
    ¾ cup whole wheat bread
       crumbs, finely ground
    3 tablespoons nutritional yeast
       (optional)
    1 cup cooked long-grain
       brown rice
    1 tablespoon low-sodium tamari
       or soy sauce
    1 teaspoon caraway seeds,
       ground
    ½ teaspoon poultry seasoning
    2 tablespoons chopped fresh
       basil leaves or 1 tablespoon
       dried basil
    1 cup alfalfa sprouts, chopped
       Oil, for greasing baking sheet
       Stone ground or Dijon
       mustard, for dipping

1. Preheat oven to 350° F. Mix together all ingredients except oil and mustard and form into 1-inch balls.

2. Place on a lightly oiled baking sheet and bake until light brown and crunchy (about 20 minutes). Serve warm with mustard.

*Makes forty-eight 1-inch balls,
8 servings.*

*Calories per serving: 300
Preparation time: 35 minutes
Baking time: 20 minutes*

SEAFOOD SPECIALTIES

Fish and shellfish can be a tasty addition to your hors d'oeuvre repertoire. The delicate flavors of seafood combine well with low-calorie marinades and wine-based sauces. Use the freshest fish available for best flavor.

PRAWNS WITH SNOW PEA BLANKETS

Use medium or jumbo prawns for this recipe. Save the marinating broth; it can be used to make a tasty dipping sauce for prawns (see Note).

    1 pound medium prawns
    2 cups white table wine
    ¼ cup Dijon mustard
    1 tablespoon chopped fresh
       tarragon or 1 teaspoon
       dried tarragon
    ½ teaspoon cayenne pepper
    2 tablespoons olive oil
    50 snow peas, for wrapping

1. In a large saucepan boil prawns in wine at high heat until prawns turn pink (3 to 4 minutes). Drain, saving wine in a large bowl. Peel and remove veins from prawns with a sharp knife.

2. Add remaining ingredients, except snow peas, to wine and toss in deveined prawns. Let marinate 4 to 8 hours or overnight.

3. Blanch snow peas briefly (about 30 seconds) in large pot of boiling water. Wrap a blanched snow pea around each marinated prawn, securing with a toothpick. Serve chilled.

Makes about 32 prawns, 8 servings.

<u>Note</u> The marinade can be thickened or reduced to a sauce by boiling it for 45 minutes at medium-high heat until one quarter the original volume.

Calories per serving: 200
Preparation time: 45 minutes
Marinating time: 4–8 hours

Meaty prawns are poached, marinated overnight in a sauce of mustard, wine, and fresh tarragon and wrapped with lightly blanched snow peas. The marinade is then reduced and served as a dipping sauce.

CHILLED PRAWNS IN BEER

This slightly spicy prawn appetizer can be a meal in itself and has become very popular in Cajun restaurants. Much of the calorie content of the beer is boiled off during the cooking process. The recipe calls for flat beer, which is simply beer that has been opened and allowed to stand at room temperature for several hours. Using one of the popular light beers will further reduce calories.

>   3 *pounds jumbo prawns,*
>   *well-rinsed*
>   4 *cups flat beer*
>   1 *small onion, minced*
>   1 *teaspoon yellow mustard seed*
>   1 *teaspoon anise seed*
>   2 *teaspoons cayenne pepper, or*
>   *to taste*
>   1 *teaspoon curry powder*
>   *Hot mustard, for dipping*
>   *(optional)*

1. In an uncovered pot boil all ingredients except hot mustard until prawns are bright pink (8 to 10 minutes), stirring occasionally.

2. Drain prawns and divide cooking liquid among small bowls. Serve prawns unpeeled—let guests peel prawns themselves and dip them in to cooking liquid. Or peel prawns and serve on wooden toothpicks with a crock of hot mustard, if used.

Serves 6 as a first course or light lunch, or 12 as an appetizer.

> *Calories per serving: 157*
> *(as 12-serving appetizer)*
> *Preparation time: 5 minutes*
> *Cooking time: 10 minutes*

CHINESE ABALONE BALLS

An exotic shellfish, abalone is ground and mixed with ginger, water chestnuts, eggs, and sesame oil, then formed into small balls and baked until crisp. (Abalone has about 100 calories per 3½-ounce serving, so go easy.) Any firm white-fleshed fish can be substituted for abalone, but abalone tastes best in this recipe.

>   ½ *pound raw abalone*
>   ¼ *cup water chestnuts, peeled*
>   2 *eggs, beaten*
>   2 *tablespoons chopped green*
>   *onion*
>   1 *teaspoon low-sodium tamari*
>   *or soy sauce*
>   ½ *teaspoon grated fresh ginger*
>   1 *teaspoon sesame oil*
>   *Finely ground whole wheat*
>   *bread crumbs, as needed*
>   *Oil, for greasing baking sheet*
>   *Tamari, for dipping*

1. Preheat oven to 400° F. *To make in food processor:* Place abalone, water chestnuts, eggs, green onion, the 1 teaspoon tamari, ginger, and sesame oil into a food processor and blend into a coarsely ground mixture. *To make by hand:* Chop abalone and water chesnuts very finely and mix with eggs, green onion, the 1 teaspoon tamari, ginger, and sesame oil.

2. Form into 1-inch balls and roll in bread crumbs.

3. Lightly grease a baking sheet and bake the abalone balls for 12 to 15 minutes, until they turn crisp and light brown. Serve warm with tamari for dipping.

Serves 6.

> *Calories per serving: 109*
> *Preparation time: 25 minutes*
> *Baking time: 15–20 minutes*

WHITE FISH SEVICHE

In the Caribbean, seviche is made with freshly caught conch or abalone. This recipe uses fresh white-fleshed fish, such as haddock or cod. Always be sure to buy fish from a reliable market and buy only fresh fish. Traditionally the raw fish is marinated for several hours in a lemon or lime juice mixture, which gives it a delicate flavor.

>   2 *red onions, finely chopped*
>   4 *to 5 cloves garlic, minced*
>   3 *red bell peppers, seeded*
>   *and chopped*
>   ¼ *cup capers*
>   ½ *cup marinated artichoke*
>   *hearts, thinly sliced*
>   2 *pounds raw white-fleshed fish,*
>   *cut into ½-inch pieces*
>   2½ *cups freshly squeezed*
>   *lime juice*
>   *Lettuce leaves, for*
>   *accompaniment*

1. Place all ingredients except lettuce leaves in a large bowl or shallow pan and toss well.

2. Cover bowl tightly with plastic wrap, place in the refrigerator, and let marinate for 4 to 8 hours or overnight. Serve slightly chilled on lettuce leaves.

Serves 12.

Note The marinade actually performs some of the cooking function usually done by heat. The citric acid in the lime juice breaks down the connective tissues of the fish and firms up protein in much the same way heat does.

> *Calories per serving: 118*
> *Preparation time: 15 minutes*
> *Marinating time: 4–8 hours*

SAVORY SPREADS AND DIPS

Spreads and dips are an excellent choice for an impromptu party. These are especially low in calories, and they can be made ahead. An elegant hors d'oeuvre table can be as easy as cutting up a few platterfuls of fresh vegetables, laying out whole grain crackers, and opening containers of these homemade dips.

FRESH SALSA

Use this mild salsa as a dip for tortilla chips or as an accompaniment to chicken, fish, and vegetarian entrées. This recipe calls for fresh chiles and tomatillos—two Mexican products found in specialty markets. If not available in your area, substitute canned chiles and red tomatoes. Fresh salsa keeps for about 10 days, covered and refrigerated.

- 3 small tomatillos
- 1 jalapeño chile, seeded and chopped
- 2 tablespoons minced garlic
- ½ cup finely chopped white onion
- 2 tablespoons olive oil
- 1 tablespoon ground fresh rosemary
- 1½ cup cored and chopped plum tomatoes
- ⅓ cup minced green bell pepper
- 2 tablespoons minced cilantro
- 3 tablespoons minced parsley
- ½ teaspoon coriander powder
- ½ teaspoon cayenne pepper, or to taste
- ½ teaspoon chili powder
- ¾ teaspoon cumin
- ¼ teaspoon cinnamon
  Freshly ground black pepper, to taste
- 1 tablespoon lime juice

In a large mixing bowl combine all ingredients, cover, and let marinate in the refrigerator overnight. Serve chilled or at room temperature.

Makes 2½ cups, 10 servings.

Calories per serving: 35
Preparation time: 20 minutes
Marinating time: 4–8 hours

BLUE CHEESE DIP WITH TOFU

This low-calorie version of everyone's favorite blue cheese dressing is thickened to turn it into a dip.

- 8 ounces soft tofu, drained
- 3 tablespoons cider vinegar
- ½ cup nonfat yogurt
- 1 teaspoon safflower oil
- 1 clove garlic, minced
- ¼ teaspoon white pepper
- 3 ounces blue cheese
  Assorted raw vegetables, for accompaniment

Purée all ingredients except raw vegetables in blender or food processor. Pour into a serving bowl and chill for several hours. Serve with raw vegetables.

Makes 2 cups, 8 servings.

Calories per serving: 72
Preparation time: 15 minutes

CURRY CHUTNEY DIP WITH HOMEMADE RUSKS

Serve this simple party dip with rusks, crackers, or vegetable sticks.

- ½ cup soft tofu
- ½ cup part-skim ricotta cheese
- ⅓ cup mango chutney, preferably without sugar
- 1 tablespoon lemon juice
- 2 teaspoons curry powder
- ¼ teaspoon cumin
- 1 teaspoon dark sesame oil

Homemade Rusks

- 1 baguette whole grain French bread

Blend all ingredients and chill for 1½ hours.

Makes 1 cup, 4 servings.

Homemade Rusks Preheat oven to 200° F. Cut baguette into thick wedges and place on ungreased baking sheet. Bake at 200° F until very crisp (about 45 minutes).

Makes 20 rusks.

Calories per serving: 25
Preparation time: 10 minutes
Baking time: 45 minutes

CONVERTING YOUR FAVORITE DIPS TO LOW-CALORIE DELICACIES

Here is an example of how to transform a favorite party dip recipe by substituting low-calorie ingredients for the fattening ones. The first recipe below is a traditional dip; the second recipe is a low-calorie version.

SALLY'S TRADITIONAL SOUR CREAM DIP

- ½ pint sour cream
- 1 teaspoon prepared horseradish
- 2 tablespoons minced chives
- 2 teaspoons minced parsley
- 1 tablespoon mayonnaise
- ¾ cup softened cream cheese
  Pinch salt

In a small bowl combine all ingredients; serve with crackers and raw vegetable sticks.

Makes approximately 2 cups, or 8 servings.

Calories per serving: 153
Preparation time: 10 minutes

SALLY'S LOW-CALORIE YOGURT DIP

- 1 cup nonfat plain yogurt
- ¾ cup blended low-fat ricotta cheese
- 2 tablespoons low-calorie mayonnaise
- 1 teaspoon prepared horseradish
- 2 tablespoons minced parsley

In a small bowl combine all ingredients; serve with crackers and raw vegetable sticks.

Makes approximately 2 cups, or 8 servings.

Calories per serving: 57
Preparation time: 10 minutes

HOLIDAY
HORS D'OEUVRE PARTY

Greek Feta Filo Cigars

*Cranberry Salsa and
Low-Calorie Cream Cheese Dip*

*Scooped-Out Green Bell Peppers
With Whole Cherry Tomatoes*

*Whole Grain Crackers and
Minibaguettes of French Bread*

Chinese Abalone Balls (see page 22)

Armenian Meatballs (see page 18)

*Filo Tart With Raspberries
(see page 122)*

Mulled Cider and Red Wine

---

*Although Christmas is
typically a time of heavy
eating and drinking, don't
get caught in the high-calorie
humdrum of heavy sit-down
dinners. For your holiday
party, serve a platter of these
low-calorie hors d'oeuvres—
your guests will appreciate
the light touch of these
international flavor treats.
The menu theme is the colors
of the season: the reds of
whole cherry tomatoes,
tomato sauce, cranberry
salsa, red wine, and
raspberries; the greens of
bell peppers, green onions,
and mulled apple cider.
Menu serves eight.*

GREEK FETA FILO CIGARS

A rectangular, paper-thin pastry dough, filo dough is most often used in strudel or baklava recipes. Try to buy unfrozen filo, because the edges of frozen filo begin to stick together when the dough thaws. Be sure the work surface is clean and dry; cover the filo you are not using with a slightly dampened kitchen towel to keep it from drying out. Once you get the knack of working with filo dough, it becomes a great resource for instantly elegant appetizers. This recipe uses very little butter, keeping the dish very low-calorie.

- 1 cup low-fat feta cheese, drained and crumbled
- ½ cup part-skim ricotta cheese
- 1 tablespoon grated Parmesan cheese
- 2 cloves garlic, minced
- 2 tablespoons minced fresh dill
- 2 eggs, lightly beaten
- ¼ teaspoon ground pepper
- 10 sheets unbuttered filo dough
- 2 tablespoons unsalted butter, melted

1. Preheat oven to 400° F. Mix cheeses, garlic, dill, eggs, and pepper until smooth. Reserve.

2. On a clean, dry surface, unroll the filo dough and stack in a pile. Using a pastry brush sprinkle the first sheet with ½ teaspoon of the butter. Repeat with second sheet and lay it on top of the first. Set aside. Repeat procedure with remaining filo dough and butter to create 5 sets of two-layered sheets.

3. Mark long side of each filo dough stack into fifths and cut into 5 equal strips, each 3 to 4 inches wide. Place a spoonful of the filling at the base of each double-layered strip and roll into a "cigar", tucking the edges in as you roll. Place cigars on a parchment-covered baking sheet. Repeat this process 4 times.

4. Bake cigars until brown (about 15 minutes). Serve hot.

Makes 25 small appetizers, approximately 8 servings.

Make-Ahead Tip The rolled, unbaked cigars, if tightly covered in plastic wrap, will keep fresh in the refrigerator for several hours.

*Calories per serving: 56
Preparation time: 30–45 minutes
Baking time: 15 minutes*

CRANBERRY SALSA AND LOW-CALORIE CREAM CHEESE DIP

A colorful dip that is often served at holiday parties, this combines the piquant flavors of cranberries, orange peel, and red onion with Neufchâtel cream cheese (which contains half the calories of regular cream cheese). The dip has a lovely pink color. Serve it in halved red or green bell peppers surrounded by raw vegetable sticks or crackers.

- 1 cup cranberries, fresh or frozen and defrosted
- 2 teaspoons grated orange peel
- ½ cup frozen orange juice concentrate, thawed
- 3 tablespoons minced red onion
- 1 tablespoon minced cilantro
- ¼ teaspoon cayenne pepper
- ½ cup low-calorie cream cheese, such as Neufchâtel
  Bell peppers, halved, seeded, veined (optional)
  Assorted raw vegetable sticks or whole grain crackers, for accompaniment (optional)

1. Blend all ingredients except bell peppers and raw vegetables in food processor or in blender until very smooth.

2. Spoon into 2 or 3 bell peppers, if used, or a glass bowl and serve chilled with raw vegetable sticks.

Makes 2½ cups, 8 servings.

*Calories per serving: 70
Preparation time: 10 minutes*

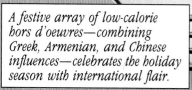

A festive array of low-calorie hors d'oeuvres—combining Greek, Armenian, and Chinese influences—celebrates the holiday season with international flair.

Good soups start with the basics: hearty stocks, flavorful fresh vegetables, lean meats, and savory herbs and spices.

Tasty Soups

S oups can be the ideal low-calorie answer to the one-dish meal or an elegant and easy way to round out a menu. Because these soups are broth or wine based rather than cream based, they are low in calories, yet flavorful due to the use of herbs and other seasonings. This chapter presents soups for all seasons, from a hearty Louisiana-style chicken gumbo (see page 28) ideal for winter evenings to a cool and refreshing melon soup (see page 36) perfect for hot summer afternoons. Instructions for sautéing vegetables for soups (see page 30) and for making several types of soup stocks (see page 31) help guide meal planning. A menu for a Mexican grilling fiesta (see page 37) completes the chapter.

SOUPS THAT MAKE A MEAL

Recipes in this section can be served as a main course, and with the addition of bread and salad, make a filling low-calorie dinner or lunch for the dieter. They are hearty and tasty, but light on rich ingredients such as cream, oils, and butter. Many begin with a sherry- or wine-based sauté, and are seasoned with herbs and spices instead of table salt.

MEXICAN CHICKEN SOUP

Inspired by a fondness for cilantro (also called coriander), this soup is a happy marriage of chicken and Mexican seasoning.

- 1 frying chicken, skinned, cut up
- 8 cups water
- 3 carrots, coarsely chopped
- 1 small russet or red potato (unpeeled), cubed
- 2 green bell peppers, julienned
- 2 large onions, sliced
- 1 large zucchini, sliced
- ¾ cup chopped cilantro, or to taste
  Herbal salt substitute and pepper, to taste
  Salsa, for accompaniment (optional)

1. In a large stockpot, place frying chicken, the water, carrots, and potato and bring to a boil. Simmer for 45 minutes.

2. Pour stock through a colander into a big bowl; let cool, pick out and discard bones and gristle from chicken.

3. Return stock, chicken meat, and cooked vegetables to stockpot and add bell pepper, onion, zucchini, and cilantro. Cook over medium heat until vegetables are tender. Test for seasoning and add salt substitute and pepper, if needed. Serve hot, with salsa if desired.

Makes 12 cups, 8 servings.

Calories per serving: 185
Preparation time: 20 minutes
Cooking time: 60 minutes

CHICKEN GUMBO LOUISIANA-STYLE

This authentic-tasting version of Louisiana gumbo was invented by a woman in a little town north of Baton Rouge. Although the recipe is adapted for low-calorie cooking, most of the original seasonings are kept intact, maintaining the stunning flavors prevalent in Creole cooking.

- 1 large frying chicken, skinned, cut up
- 2 tablespoons flour
  Herbal salt substitute and pepper, to taste
  Oil, for greasing
- 1 large onion, chopped
- 1 teaspoon safflower oil
- 5 green onions, chopped
- 1 large clove garlic, mashed
- ½ dried chile (piquito variety)
- 1 bay leaf
- 1 sprig fresh thyme
- ¼ cup chopped parsley
- 7 cups defatted Chicken Stock (see page 31)
- 2 cups cooked brown rice
  Cayenne pepper, to taste

1. Preheat oven to 350° F. Coat chicken pieces with flour and sprinkle with salt substitute and pepper. Place on a lightly greased baking sheet and bake, turning once, until well browned (about 20 minutes).

2. While chicken is baking, sauté onion in safflower oil in a large heavy stockpot or Dutch oven. Cook until soft, then add green onion, garlic, chile, bay leaf, thyme, and parsley. Cook 5 minutes.

3. Add stock, rice, and baked chicken pieces. Simmer until chicken is tender (about 1 hour). Sprinkle with cayenne.

Makes 12 cups, 8 servings.

Calories per serving: 210
Preparation time: 35 minutes
Cooking time: 90 minutes

MARY'S BOURRIDE

Bourride is a French fish soup that has a variety of exquisite seasonings, such as saffron, orange peel, and fennel. (Traditionally a garlic mayonnaise, called aioli, is added at the end, but it is omitted here to minimize calories.) Serve Mary's Bourride when you happen upon some fresh fish (any white-fleshed fish, such as cod or halibut, will do) and want to invite a lot of friends to dinner.

- 2 teaspoons olive oil
- ½ large onion, sliced
- 1 medium carrot, sliced into rounds
- 1 large leek, cleaned and sliced into rounds
- 2 ripe tomatoes, cored and coarsely chopped
- 6 cups defatted Fish Stock (see page 31) or water
- ½ cup dry vermouth or dry white wine
- 1 bay leaf
- ¼ teaspoon dried thyme
- 1 clove garlic, halved
- ¼ teaspoon chopped orange peel
- 2 pinches saffron
- ¼ teaspoon fennel seed
- 1½ pounds fresh, firm-fleshed fish
  Herbal salt substitute, to taste
- 6 to 8 slices French bread

1. In a large stockpot over medium-high heat, heat oil; add onion and sauté until onion is very soft. Add carrot, leek, and tomatoes, and sauté 5 minutes, stirring frequently.

2. Add stock, vermouth, bay leaf, thyme, garlic, orange peel, saffron, and fennel seed. Bring to a boil. Simmer until vegetables are tender (about 10 minutes).

3. Wash fish and pat dry; remove all bones and cut fish into 3-inch chunks. Add fish to stockpot and cook just until fish flakes.

4. Season to taste with salt substitute and serve hot over sliced bread in large soup bowls.

Makes 12 cups, 8 servings.

Calories per serving: 296
Preparation time: 20 minutes
Cooking time: 20 minutes

SOUTHERN ITALIAN VEGETABLE SOUP

This soup has a hearty flavor and is thick enough to be served as a complete meal.

- 1 teaspoon olive oil
- 1 medium onion, sliced
- 1 medium carrot, sliced
- 2 medium red potatoes (unpeeled), cubed
- 1 stalk celery with leaves, chopped
- 1 clove garlic, chopped
- 2 zucchini, sliced
- 1 cup chopped green cabbage
- 1 large tomato, cored and chopped
- ¼ cup uncooked macaroni
- 4 cups defatted Chicken Stock (see page 31)
- 1 cup cooked navy beans (approximately ½ cup raw)
- 1 teaspoon dried basil
- ¼ cup chopped parsley
  Herbal salt substitute and pepper, to taste

1. In a large stockpot, heat oil over medium heat. Add onion and slowly sauté until onion is soft and translucent. Add carrot and potatoes and cook 3 minutes.

2. Add celery, garlic, zucchini, cabbage, and tomato and cook 5 minutes more, stirring frequently. Add macaroni, stock, beans, basil, parsley, salt substitute, and pepper; bring to a boil.

3. Lower heat to simmer, cover, and continue cooking for 35 minutes. Taste for seasoning and serve hot.

Makes 8 cups, 6 servings.

Note You can use the listed fresh vegetables or substitute others. Cook up the beans either at the same time as the rest of the soup or the night before. As an added benefit, this soup freezes well.

> *Calories per serving: 200*
> *Preparation time: 25 minutes*
> *Cooking time: 40 minutes*

Bourride is a hearty fish soup from southern France that is redolent of orange, fennel, and thyme. Serve it with crusty baguettes, a light green salad, and lemon- or lime-flavored sparkling water.

SAUTÉING VEGETABLES FOR SOUPS

All the vegetable-based soup recipes presented in this chapter follow a general order of sautéing to keep the vegetables from losing flavor. Always start with a little oil or sherry in the bottom of the stockpot and let it heat until very hot. Before sautéing, be sure that the vegetables are dry to prevent steam from forming when they are added to the oil. This is first a matter of safety for the cook; moisture that comes in contact with the hot oil splatters wildly. In addition, it is theorized that steam prevents the oil from sealing the food.

Add vegetables in the order given below, stirring until each is coated completely with oil or sherry. Cook until vegetables soften and brighten in color.

1. Onions, green onions, leeks, shallots, and other vegetables of the onion family

2. Carrots, beets, turnips, jicama, ginger, and other root vegetables

3. Cabbage, celery, bok choy, and other stalked vegetables

4. Peppers, squash, beans, peas, and other vine vegetables

5. Tomatoes

6. Mushrooms

7. Garlic

8. Fresh herbs

9. Dried herbs

Following this general order helps the soup develop a full, robust flavor—and as a side benefit lets you skip the salt.

BEAN AND BARLEY SOUP

A hearty addition to any meal, this thick bean soup should be made the day before for best flavor. Be sure to plan time to precook the dried beans (for a faster version, use canned, unsalted beans that are already cooked). Try making a double recipe and freezing half for later use.

¼ cup dry sherry
2 teaspoons olive oil
1 cup sliced onion
2 cups sliced fresh mushrooms, such as domestic white, chanterelles, or shiitake
1 cup diced, unpeeled red potato
1 cup shredded carrot
1 teaspoon minced fresh basil
1 tablespoon minced garlic
2 cups cooked pinto beans
1 cup raw barley
4 cups defatted Chicken Stock (see page 31)
2 tablespoons minced parsley
1 teaspoon herbal salt substitute
⅛ teaspoon cayenne pepper

1. In a heavy stockpot heat sherry and oil to simmering, then add onion. Stir well and cook over medium-high heat until soft but not too browned (5 to 8 minutes).

2. Add mushrooms, potato, carrot, basil, and garlic. Cook, stirring frequently, until mushrooms begin to weep moisture (about 8 minutes). Add beans and barley and cook for 2 more minutes.

3. Add stock, parsley, salt substitute, and cayenne. Bring to a boil, then lower heat to simmer. Cover pot and cook over medium heat until barley is tender (about 30 minutes). Serve hot.

Makes 8 cups, about 8 servings.

> *Calories per serving: 182*
> *Preparation time: 20 minutes*
> *Cooking time: 45 minutes*

LIGHT AND EASY SOUPS

Perfect for a hot summer day, or as a simple make-ahead first course to an elegant dinner, these light and easy soups are a bonus when you have little time. Chilled soups are best served before the main meal, as their flavors are more delicate than those of hot soups. A light soup acts much like an appetizer—it teases and stimulates the palate but does not overload the stomach.

LEEK AND MUSHROOM SOUP

In France, where this soup is a favorite, leeks are a popular vegetable. This soup relies on their light but distinctive flavor.

1 teaspoon safflower oil
¼ cup sherry
5 thick leeks, cleaned and sliced into rounds
2 cups thinly sliced fresh mushrooms
4 cups defatted Chicken Stock (see page 31)
2 teaspoons minced fresh chervil or parsley, or 1 teaspoon dried chervil or parsley
1 teaspoon dried basil

1. In a stockpot heat oil and sherry; add leeks and cook over medium-high heat until they are very soft and beginning to brown.

2. Add 1 cup of the mushrooms and cook over low heat until mushrooms weep moisture.

3. Add stock, chervil, and basil. Bring to a boil and cook 25 minutes over medium heat.

4. Add remaining mushrooms and simmer 5 minutes longer. Serve hot.

Makes 8 cups, 5 servings.

> *Calories per serving: 124*
> *Preparation time: 15 minutes*
> *Cooking time: 35 minutes*

KOMBU MISO SOUP

A delicious vegetarian version of the popular miso (soy paste) soup that is served in restaurants, this includes a flavorful Japanese sea vegetable called *kombu*, which can be found in most Asian food stores. The recipe also calls for red and white miso.

For a graceful presentation, sliver green onion ends and float them on the surface of each bowl of soup. Top with black sesame seeds, which are also available at Asian markets and general supermarkets.

> 3 pieces kombu seaweed, dried
> (about 9 in. total)
> 6 cups water
> ½ cup red miso
> ½ cup white miso
> 4 ounces firm tofu, cut into
> ¼-inch cubes
> 1 green onion, minced
> Low-sodium tamari or soy
> sauce, to taste (optional)

1. In a large stockpot, simmer kombu in the water for 30 minutes, then strain. Discard cooked kombu.

2. Heat kombu stock to boiling. Remove 1 cup of stock from stockpot and dissolve red and white misos into it, blending carefully with the back of a large spoon until all lumps are gone. Return mixture to stockpot.

3. Add tofu and green onion to stock. Turn off heat and let stand 3 minutes to heat tofu. Taste for seasoning and add tamari (if used).

Makes 7½ cups, 6 servings.

Calories per serving: 135
Preparation time: 5 minutes
Cooking time: 40 minutes

Basics

HOW TO MAKE SOUP STOCKS

Regardless of the base—vegetable, beef, fish, or chicken—do not boil the stock. Instead, simmer slowly. Boiling stock brings out acids and may also increase bitter tastes in vegetables and other bases.

VEGETARIAN STOCK

Vegetarian stock can be refrigerated, covered, for up to ten days, or frozen for up to five months.

> 1 cup vegetable of choice
> (see Note)
> 4 cups water

In a stockpot combine ingredients; simmer over low heat for 2 hours, then strain.

Makes 4 cups.

Note Because the following vegetables leave an unpleasant flavor, do not use them to make Vegetarian Stock: cucumbers, lettuce, spinach, carrot or beet greens, peppers.

BEEF STOCK

Beef stock can be refrigerated, covered, for up to four days, and frozen for up to three months.

> 3 pounds veal or beef bones
> 1 teaspoon safflower oil
> Water, to cover
> 1 stalk celery
> 1 onion, quartered
> 1 bay leaf
> 1 carrot

In a stockpot brown veal bones in 1 teaspoon safflower oil. Then add remaining ingredients, simmer 3 hours, and strain.

Makes 4 cups.

FISH STOCK

Fish stock can be refrigerated, covered, for up to five days, and frozen for up to two months.

> 2 pounds fishtails, fish heads,
> shells from shrimp, or
> fish bones
> Water, to cover
> 1 stalk celery
> 1 onion, quartered
> 1 bay leaf
> 1 carrot

In a large stockpot combine all ingredients; simmer 1½ hours and then strain.

Makes 4 to 6 cups.

CHICKEN STOCK

Chicken stock can be refrigerated, covered, for up to six days and frozen for up to two months (see Note).

> 2 pounds chicken bones, back,
> and neck
> Water, to cover
> 1 stalk celery
> 1 onion, quartered
> 1 bay leaf
> 1 carrot

In a large stockpot combine chicken bones, back, and neck and the water. Add celery, onion, bay leaf, and carrot. Simmer over low heat 1½ hours. Strain.

Makes 4 to 6 cups.

Note To remove fat: Allow stock to chill for 2 hours. Fat will separate and rise to the top. Scoop fat off with spoon and discard. Remaining stock may be used in recipes calling for defatted chicken stock.

Rich tasting, but low in calories, Curried Acorn Squash Bisque is certainly harvest fare—a purée of baked acorn squash and red bell peppers, with sherry, ginger, pepper, and curry spices.

CURRIED ACORN SQUASH BISQUE

This bisque, adapted from a high-calorie recipe, is a deliciously seasoned soup, with seven flavorings that surpass the taste of the finest curry powder. Serve it with a light chicken or fish dish, crusty bread, and a fruit dessert.

> 2 small acorn squash
> 1 teaspoon safflower oil
> ½ cup minced onion
> 2 cloves garlic, minced
> 1 red bell pepper, seeded and finely diced
> ⅓ cup dry sherry
> 2½ cups defatted Chicken Stock (see page 31)
> 1 cup freshly squeezed orange juice
> ½ teaspoon ground cumin
> ½ teaspoon ground coriander
> 1 teaspoon grated fresh ginger
> ¼ teaspoon dry mustard
>   Herbal salt substitute, to taste
> ¼ teaspoon cayenne pepper
> ¼ teaspoon white pepper
> ¼ cup plain, nonfat yogurt

1. Preheat oven to 350° F. Split squash lengthwise, leaving in the seeds (to help the squash steam more quickly due to moisture content). Place halves, split side down, on an aluminum-foil–lined baking sheet. Bake until soft (about 40 minutes).

2. Scoop out squash seeds and discard. Scoop flesh from shells and mash well; set aside. Discard shells.

3. In a large stockpot, heat oil; add onion and sauté over medium heat until onion is soft.

4. Add garlic, bell pepper, and sherry; cook 5 minutes. Add reserved squash, stock, orange juice, cumin, coriander, ginger, dry mustard, salt substitute, cayenne, and white pepper.

5. Bring to a boil, lower heat, cover, and simmer for 35 minutes. Purée soup and stir in yogurt. Taste for seasoning and serve hot.

Makes 6 cups, 6 servings.

Calories per serving: 131
Preparation time: 20 minutes
Cooking time: 75 minutes

HOT AND SOUR SOUP

The trick with this soup is to attain a delicate balance between the savory stock, spicy pepper, sour vinegar, and mushroom flavors.

- 8 cups defatted Chicken Stock (see page 31)
- ½ cup dried black mushrooms, such as Japanese shiitake
- 1 teaspoon sesame oil
- 1 tablespoon sake
- ¼ cup minced onion
- 8 ounces firm tofu, cubed
- 3 tablespoons arrowroot mixed with ½ cup cold water
- 3½ tablespoons rice vinegar
- 1 beaten egg
- 3 teaspoons low-sodium tamari or soy sauce
- ¼ teaspoon cayenne pepper
- ⅛ teaspoon freshly ground black pepper

1. In a large stockpot, heat stock. Add dried mushrooms and simmer for 15 minutes.

2. Strain out mushrooms, leaving stock simmering on the stove. Cut off and discard mushroom stems. Slice tops thinly and return to stockpot.

3. In a small skillet heat sesame oil and sake; add onion and sauté slowly until onion is very soft. Add onion and any pan liquor to stock in stockpot.

4. Stir in tofu, arrowroot mixture, vinegar, egg, tamari, cayenne, and black pepper; cook until egg forms into ribbons and soup thickens slightly from arrowroot (about 1 minute). Serve hot.

Makes 10 cups, 8 servings.

Calories per serving: 121
Preparation time: 10 minutes
Cooking time: 25 minutes

SHOMINI ABOOR
Turkish spinach soup

This is an easily prepared, low-calorie soup, but don't let the simple ingredients or directions deceive you—this spinach soup is delicious. This soup is served in the Middle East as a light meal or as a first course before lamb or beef. Try it with the Marinated Beef Kabobs on page 82.

- 4 cups defatted Chicken Stock (see page 31)
- 1½ cups chopped fresh spinach
- ½ cup raw bulgur
- ½ cup raw lentils
- 1 clove garlic, mashed
  Herbal salt substitute, to taste
- 2 cups peeled and chopped fresh tomatoes
- 2 tablespoons tomato paste
- 2 tablespoons dried basil

1. In a stockpot bring stock to a boil. Add spinach, bulgur, and lentils. Bring to a boil again; lower heat; cover; and simmer for 25 to 30 minutes.

2. Add garlic, salt substitute, tomatoes, and tomato paste; cook until lentils are soft (about 30 minutes). Add basil during last 5 minutes of cooking time.

3. Taste for seasoning and serve hot.

Makes 8 cups, 6 servings.

Calories per serving: 155
Preparation time: 10 minutes
Cooking time: 60 minutes

FRENCH-STYLE CREAM OF BROCCOLI SOUP

The flavor of this light and simple soup depends on peak of the season herbs and vegetables. It makes a pleasant first course or a light summer luncheon with a garden salad, crusty whole wheat bread, and a light fruit dessert such as Wine-Basted Pears (see page 115).

- 1 teaspoon safflower oil
- ½ medium onion, finely chopped
- ½ cup firmly packed chopped celery leaves and stalk
- 2 large stalks of broccoli (stems included), chopped
- 1 cup defatted Chicken Stock (see page 31)
- 2 cups nonfat milk
- 2 teaspoons chopped fresh dill
- 1 teaspoon herbal salt substitute
- 1 teaspoon chopped fresh basil
- ½ teaspoon very finely minced fresh rosemary leaves
- ½ cup rolled oats

1. In a stockpot heat oil; add onion and sauté over medium heat until onion is soft and translucent.

2. Add celery, broccoli, and stock; cover and cook over low heat until broccoli is bright green (about 8 minutes).

3. Remove to blender; add milk, dill, salt substitute, basil, rosemary, and oats; purée. Return to stockpot and heat through. Taste for seasoning and serve hot.

Makes 6 cups, 6 servings.

Calories per serving: 85
Preparation time: 20 minutes
Cooking time: 10 minutes

... ON FREEZING SOUPS

Soups freeze better than almost any other kind of cooked food. You can use the freezer during several stages of soup making. Here are some tips.

☐ If you're planning to freeze a soup, undercook it just a little, so that the vegetables stay crisp and bright in color.

☐ Before freezing let the cooked soup come to room temperature, preferably in a cool spot.

☐ Pour soup into food-grade plastic containers or doubled sealable plastic bags; fill only three fourths of the way (the soup will expand when frozen). It's best to package soup in 2-cup portions, so you won't have leftovers.

☐ Freeze solid. Do not refreeze any meat- or fish-based soups, since they can develop bacteria during the freezing process.

☐ Try freezing homemade broths (see How to Make Soup Stocks, page 31) in ice cube trays: Pour hot soup into plastic or metal trays, freeze, then transfer the cubes to a heavy-weight sealable plastic bag. This method is ideal for cooking small portions—four cubes, when defrosted, make approximately ½ cup of broth.

☐ For an instant lunch: Sauté ½ cup mixed vegetables, such as onion, carrot, celery, cabbage, and red bell pepper in 1 teaspoon olive oil. Add 4 frozen cubes of homemade stock, cover pot, and let cook on medium heat until stock is defrosted (about 5 minutes). Simply season to taste with fresh herbs, herbal salt substitute, and freshly ground pepper, and you have soup for a quick lunch.

GINGERED CAULIFLOWER SOUP

This light soup, reminiscent of Asian cooking, is thickened with rolled oats, which have no taste but create a wonderful creamy texture without the calories of cream. The jicama (pronounced HEE-ki-muh), a Mexican root vegetable, can be replaced by water chestnuts. As a nutritional bonus, the rolled oats provide a good source of fiber.

1 teaspoon safflower oil
¼ cup dry sherry
1 medium onion, minced
2 teaspoons grated fresh ginger
2 cups chopped cauliflower
4 cups defatted Chicken Stock or Vegetarian Stock (see page 31)
1 cup julienned jicama
¼ cup rolled oats
½ cup minced green onion, including greens
1 teaspoon dark sesame oil
Herbal salt substitute and pepper, to taste

1. In a stockpot heat oil and sherry; add onion and ginger and sauté over medium heat until soft.

2. Add cauliflower and cook 3 minutes, stirring. Add stock, jicama, and oats; bring to a boil. Lower heat, cover, and simmer for 25 minutes.

3. Purée cauliflower mixture in blender. Return to pot and add green onion and sesame oil. Heat through. Add salt substitute and pepper and serve hot.

Makes 8 cups, 6 servings.

> *Calories per serving: 87*
> *Preparation time: 25 minutes*
> *Cooking time: 45 minutes*

GARLIC SOUP GILROY-STYLE

Gilroy, located east of Santa Cruz, California, is the "Garlic Capital" of the world. Each year the town conducts a garlic festival that fills the air with the aroma of roasting garlic. This Gilroy recipe simmers the hometown spice to bring out its sweetness.

1 teaspoon safflower oil
1 cup dry white wine
1 medium onion, finely chopped
5 bulbs of garlic, wrapped in cheesecloth and mashed
4 cups defatted Chicken Stock (see page 31)
2 bay leaves, crushed
½ teaspoon dried thyme
¼ teaspoon dried marjoram
4 sprigs parsley, chopped
Herbal salt substitute and pepper, to taste
½ cup nonfat milk

1. In a stockpot heat oil and wine; add onion and sauté over medium heat until onion is soft.

2. Add garlic wrapped in cheesecloth, stock, bay leaves, thyme, marjoram, and parsley. Bring to a boil; lower heat, cover, and simmer for 45 minutes. (Do not let soup boil rapidly or garlic will become bitter.)

3. Remove cheesecloth packet of garlic. Take soft, cooked garlic from cloth and force it through a sieve, leaving the papery skins behind; add mashed garlic to soup.

4. Add salt substitute, pepper, and milk; heat through and serve.

Makes 6 cups, 6 servings.

> *Calories per serving: 110*
> *Preparation time: 15 minutes*
> *Cooking time: 55 minutes*

PESTO SUMMER VEGETABLE SOUP

This French summer soup depends heavily on fresh, tasty produce, which is usually best when the garden is at its peak. Don't be afraid to substitute other seasonal vegetables for the ones listed below.

    1 teaspoon olive oil
    ⅓ cup sliced onion
    ½ cup diced red potato
    ½ cup sliced green beans
    ½ cup sliced zucchini
    ¼ cup chopped celery leaves
    ½ cup peeled and chopped tomato
    1 cup cooked navy beans (approximately ½ cup raw)
    ⅛ teaspoon saffron
    ½ teaspoon pepper
    4 cups defatted Chicken Stock or Vegetarian Stock (see page 31)
    2 tablespoons tomato paste
      Herbal salt substitute, to taste

Pesto

    2 cloves garlic, minced
    1 cup chopped fresh basil leaves
    ¼ cup walnuts, very finely chopped
    2 tablespoons grated Parmesan cheese

1. In a stockpot heat oil; add onion and sauté over medium heat until onion is soft.

2. Add potato, green beans, zucchini, celery leaves, tomato, navy beans, saffron, pepper, and stock. Bring to a boil, cover, and simmer for 35 minutes, stirring occasionally.

3. Stir in tomato paste and Pesto; season to taste with salt substitute..

Makes 7 cups, 6 servings.

Pesto In a blender, combine garlic, basil, walnuts, and cheese, and pureé.

Makes 1½ cups, 6 servings.

Calories per serving: 170
Preparation time: 25 minutes
Cooking time: 45 minutes

Alive with the flavors of midsummer, Pesto Summer Vegetable Soup is delicately seasoned with fresh basil, garlic, and, if desired, herbal salt substitute. Serve with bread sticks.

SUMMER MELON SOUP WITH LIME

A very refreshing dessert or first-course, this soup can also be an invigorating beverage in the hot summer weather. This soup uses three types of melon—cantaloupe, honeydew, and casaba—but cantaloupe can be substituted for the casaba if necessary.

    2 cups peeled, seeded, and
       chopped ripe cantaloupe
    1 cup peeled, seeded, and
       chopped ripe honeydew
    2 cups peeled, seeded, and
       chopped ripe casaba
    ⅓ cup freshly squeezed lime juice
    1 teaspoon honey
    ¼ cup nonfat, plain yogurt
    ¼ cup chopped fresh mint leaves,
       for garnish

In a food processor or blender, purée all ingredients except mint leaves. Chill thoroughly and serve garnished with mint in small glass bowls.

Makes 6 cups, 6 servings.

> *Calories per serving: 56*
> *Preparation time: 20 minutes*
> *Chilling time: 60 minutes*

FRESH TOMATO SOUP WITH DILL

The best time to try this recipe is when tomatoes are at their summer ripest. Serve chilled or heated.

    1 teaspoon safflower oil
    ¼ cup dry sherry
    2 cups finely minced onion
    1 tablespoon minced garlic
    ½ cup minced red bell pepper
    5 large ripe beefsteak tomatoes,
       peeled and coarsely chopped
    2 cups defatted Chicken Stock
       (see page 31)
    2 tablespoons chopped fresh
       dill
       Herbal salt substitute and
       pepper, to taste

1. In a stockpot over low heat, warm oil and sherry. Add onion and sauté slowly, until onion is soft.

Chilled Curried Zucchini Soup combines puréed zucchini, green onions, curry spices, and low-fat buttermilk for a refreshing summer treat. Here it is accompanied by a citrus salad tossed with a tangy vinaigrette dressing.

COOL AND REFRESHING SOUPS

The main ingredients in these soups are fresh fruits or vegetables; the soups are cooked slightly, seasoned subtly, and then refrigerated for several hours to blend the flavors. Use only the freshest, ripest fruits and vegetables, since the just-picked flavor is essential to the success of these soups.

2. Add garlic and red pepper; cook 3 minutes, stirring. Add tomatoes and cook 5 minutes more.

3. Add stock and dill and bring to a boil. Lower heat, cover, and simmer for 45 minutes. Add salt substitute and pepper, and serve.

Makes 8 cups, 8 servings.

Calories per serving: 67
Preparation time: 25 minutes
Cooking time: 60 minutes

CHILLED CURRIED ZUCCHINI SOUP

This refreshing and delicate soup is ideal for a light summer lunch. Serve it with a large salad of greens, orange sections, and radishes, tossed with a vinaigrette dressing.

    2 teaspoons safflower oil
    1 large onion, sliced
    3 green onions, minced
    3 to 4 medium-sized zucchini,
      sliced, plus grated zucchini,
      for garnish
    1 tablespoon curry powder
    1 tablespoon ground cumin
    2 cups water
    3 cups low-fat buttermilk
      Herbal salt substitute and
      pepper, to taste

1. In a large stockpot, heat oil; add onion and sauté over medium heat until onion is soft. Add green onion and zucchini and continue cooking over medium heat until zucchini is limp.

2. Add curry powder, cumin, and the water and cook for 5 minutes over medium heat.

3. Add buttermilk; transfer soup to blender and blend to a smooth purée. Add salt substitute and pepper; chill. Serve garnished with grated zucchini.

Makes 6 cups, 8 servings.

Calories per serving: 68
Preparation time: 15 minutes
Cooking time: 10 minutes
Chilling time: 60 minutes

---

menu

*Low-Calorie Guacamole Dip
With Raw Vegetable Basket*

Iced Sangria

Mushroom Kabobs

Green Gazpacho

*Mexican Baked Fish in Salsa Verde
(see page 91)*

*Mexican Bean Salad
(see page 47)*

*Platter of Sliced Papaya, Mango,
Melon, and Kiwifruit*

Spicy Green Gazpacho and Baked Fish in Salsa Verde add the zing of fresh chiles to this outdoor south-of-the-border menu. These recipes are four-star but deceptively low in calories. Offer a selection of sparkling water or add fruit juice to red wine and chill for an icy sangria. Preheat the grill or barbecue about one hour before dinner, so that the coals will be ready when you are. Most of the menu can be prepared ahead and reheated at the last minute. Chill the fruit for dessert and then slice onto chilled platters and garnish with lime wedges. Menu serves from four to six.

LOW-CALORIE GUACAMOLE DIP WITH RAW VEGETABLE BASKET

Most guacamole dishes are made with oil, mayonnaise, and lots of fat-rich avocados and are high in calories. This is a lower-calorie version that blends avocado with low-calorie farmer cheese, but tastes just as good. Use hard-skinned Hass avocados (black skin indicates ripeness), so the shells can be cut in half, scooped out, and stuffed. Believe it or not, an avocado pit stuffed into the center of a bowl of guacamole prevents guacamole from turning brown. It really works, but be prepared to explain to your friends why the pit is there.

    2 ripe avocados (preferably
      Hass), scooped out, with meat,
      shells, and pits reserved
    2 tablespoons fresh lemon juice
    ½ cup farmer cheese
    3 tablespoons salsa
    ¼ cup cooked shrimp meat
    3 cloves garlic, minced
    1 tablespoon minced cilantro,
      plus chopped cilantro, for
      garnish (optional)
    1 head curly endive or lettuce,
      separated into leaves
    1 cup carrot sticks
    1 cup whole cherry tomatoes
    1 cup raw cauliflower florets

In a blender or food processor, place avocado meat, lemon juice, cheese, salsa, shrimp, garlic, and minced cilantro; purée. Spoon into scooped-out avocado shells. Bury a pit in the center of each shell. Line a platter with endive and on it arrange stuffed shells surrounded by carrot sticks, cherry tomatoes, and cauliflower florets. Garnish with chopped cilantro, if desired. Serve slightly chilled or at room temperature.

Serves 4 to 6.

Calories per serving: 136
Preparation time: 25 minutes

MUSHROOM KABOBS

Grilling, a popular outdoor summer activity, can easily be incorporated into your low-calorie meal planning. These vegetarian kabobs can be assembled and marinated the night before your meal or party.

Mushrooms absorb the flavor of olive oil well and grill easily. They are combined on bamboo skewers with cherry tomatoes, onion, bell pepper, and pineapple chunks for a colorful finger food.

- 2 cups whole button mushrooms
- 24 cherry tomatoes (see Note)
- 1 red onion, cut into 1-inch chunks
- 2 large red bell peppers, seeded and cut into 1-inch squares
- 1 cup pineapple chunks, unsweetened
- 2 teaspoons olive oil, for brushing

1. Prepare mesquite grill, if used. Presoak bamboo skewers in salted water (1 tablespoon salt per cup of water) for 15 minutes to prevent burning on grill. Arrange vegetables on bamboo skewers, alternating colors and shapes, until you have filled 12 skewers. Brush lightly with olive oil.

2. Grill kabobs briefly over hot coals or under a broiler, turning frequently until lightly browned and slightly crisp (about 15 minutes). Serve warm.

Makes 12 kabobs, serves 4 to 6.

Note You may want to add the cherry tomatoes near the end of grilling time to help keep their shape.

Calories per serving: 60
Preparation time: 20 minutes
Cooking time: 15 minutes

GREEN GAZPACHO

A traditional Spanish chilled vegetable soup, gazpacho is sometimes blended to a purée, sometimes left chunky. Gazpacho is usually a tomato-based soup but here is a new version made with fresh green vegetables and a chicken stock flavored with snow peas.

- 6 cups snow peas
- 3 cups defatted Chicken Stock (see page 31)
- 1 small onion, finely minced
- 2 cloves garlic, pressed
- ½ cup chopped green bell pepper
- 1 small jalapeño chile, seeded and finely chopped
- ¾ cup chopped celery stalk and leaves
- 2 teaspoons lemon juice, preferably fresh
- 1 teaspoon lime juice, preferably fresh
- ½ teaspoon dried tarragon
- ½ teaspoon ground cumin
- ⅛ teaspoon cayenne pepper, or to taste
  Herbal salt substitute, to taste
  Chopped fresh tomatillos, for garnish

1. In a stockpot place snow peas and stock; bring to a boil. Lower heat and simmer 35 minutes. Strain out snow peas and reserve (see Note).

2. Add onion, garlic, bell pepper, jalapeño, celery, lemon juice, lime juice, tarragon, and cumin; chill. Add cayenne and salt substitute and serve cold, garnished with chopped tomatillos.

Makes 5 cups, 4 to 6 servings.

Note If desired, purée or chop the cooked snow peas and add to soup for a sweeter flavor.

Calories per serving: 92
Preparation time: 20 minutes
Cooking time: 45 minutes
Chilling time: 2 hours

The coals are hot, and the first course is marinated mushroom kabobs followed by Green Gazpacho and Mexican Baked Fish in Salsa Verde. Olé!

Garden-fresh greens are essential for creating satisfying salads. Accompany them with rich-tasting but low-fat dressings and eye-catching garnishes.

Fresh Salads

Salads, of course, are great for dieting, but everyone knows they can get boring. In this chapter you'll find not only a variety of fresh green salads, but also fruit, pasta, bean, rice, and grain salad recipes from all over the world. Try a taco salad from Mexico (see page 43), a tabbouleh from Lebanon (see page 44), an Indonesian peanut slaw (see page 44), a German potato salad (see page 45), or Szechwan noodles from the Far East (see page 47). The chapter also presents tips for creating your own low-calorie salad dressings (see page 42) and special secrets on serving salads to guests. All the dishes in a special make-ahead menu (see page 50) can be prepared the morning of or even the night before a gourmet dinner party for six.

... ON LOW-CALORIE SALAD DRESSINGS

Did you know that just two table-spoons of an ordinary salad dressing can increase your salad calorie count by almost 200? Luckily you can still enjoy tasty dressings without adding a lot of calories to a meal.

☐ In creamy dressings substitute nonfat, plain yogurt or low-calorie mayonnaise for sour cream, mayonnaise, or heavy cream. Or, use one third the amount of oil and beat it to a froth with a whisk or in a blender.

☐ Eliminate half the oil and substitute a flavored vinegar. Simply heat to the boiling point 2 cups of apple cider vinegar. Remove from heat and add one of the following flavorings: two sprigs of fresh herbs, such as tarragon, thyme, or basil; 3 to 4 peeled cloves of garlic plus 1 teaspoon of cracked peppercorns; or ¼ cup raspberries or blueberries plus 1 teaspoon honey. Let the flavored vinegar marinate for 48 hours at room temperature, strain, and use.

☐ Purée fresh vegetables to add flavor and thickness to dressings. You can use celery, tomato, parsley, red bell pepper, chives, watercress, or green onion.

☐ Use soft tofu in place of sour cream, olive oil, or mayonnaise. Blend until smooth and chill slightly before serving.

☐ Try part-skim buttermilk and cottage cheese in dressings. A very simple, but low-calorie dressing can be made from blended buttermilk or cottage cheese, a little lemon juice or vinegar, garlic, chives, and parsley.

SALADS THAT MAKE A MEAL

When you're really hungry and you want a big bowl of salad that is as attractive to the eye as to the palate, try one of these scrumptious recipes. These salads are designed as side dishes that can also be a meal for a single hungry person. They are hearty yet light, simple to prepare, and filling enough for a main dish.

AUDREY'S SPINACH SALAD

A delicate curried dressing anoints this tasty salad, making it appropriate for special occasions. Serve in summer with a chilled soup and crusty bread. The dressing can be made up to four days in advance; refrigerate it in a tightly covered container.

      8 cups washed and torn
         spinach leaves
      1 small red onion, sliced into
         thin rings (see Note)
      1 red Delicious apple, cored and
         chopped, sprinkled with
         1 teaspoon lemon juice
      2 tablespoons currants
      1 teaspoon olive oil
      1 clove garlic, minced
      2 cups plain, nonfat yogurt
      1 tablespoon curry powder
      1 tablespoon frozen apple juice
         concentrate
      ½ teaspoon ground cardamom
      ¼ teaspoon cayenne pepper
      ½ teaspoon grated fresh ginger

1. Place spinach in a large salad bowl. Decorate with onion rings, apple, and currants.

2. Place all other ingredients in blender and purée. Pour over spinach salad and serve.

Serves 6.

Note To make red onion taste sweeter, place the rings in a bowl of ice water for 25 minutes before using to draw out bitter acids.

Calories per serving: 98
Preparation time: 20 minutes

CHILLED CURRIED CAULIFLOWER SALAD WITH RAISINS

Here's a great salad recipe discovered by chilling leftover cauliflower and pea curry. This version adapted for low-calorie cooking is made with raisins and strips of fresh bell pepper. As a cold curry recipe, it is a twist on the traditional hot Indian curry dishes. You will find that the hot peppers somehow have a cooling effect on the body. It's sweet and succulent—ideal for summer entertaining on your porch or patio.

      4 cups broken cauliflower tops
      1 cup julienned carrots
      1 cup seeded and julienned red
         bell pepper
      ½ cup apple juice
      1 tablespoon dark sesame oil
      2 cloves garlic, minced
      2 tablespoons curry powder
      ½ teaspoon cinnamon
     1½ teaspoons whole yellow
         mustard seed
      2 teaspoons honey
      ½ cup raisins
         Lettuce leaves, for lining plates

1. Steam cauliflower, carrot, and bell pepper in apple juice until tender. Drain and toss with oil, garlic, curry powder, cinnamon, mustard seed, honey, and raisins.

2. Cover and chill for 2 hours or overnight. To serve, line plates with lettuce leaves and top with cauliflower mixture.

Serves 6.

Calories per serving: 115
Preparation time: 25 minutes
Chilling time: 2 hours

TACO SALAD

If you're a fan of Mexican food, especially the piquant flavor of tacos, you'll love this salad. Chili-seasoned tofu is mixed with typical taco fillings and served over baked corn chips. Taco Salad is festive with Green Gazpacho (see page 39).

    2 cups crumbled firm tofu
    2 teaspoons ground cumin
    2 tablespoons chopped cilantro
    ½ teaspoon chili powder
    2 teaspoons herbal salt
      substitute
    ¼ teaspoon pepper
    2 teaspoons safflower oil
    6 corn tortillas
    3 cups torn leaf lettuce, such as
      romaine or green leaf
    3 large, ripe tomatoes, cored
      and coarsely chopped
    ½ cup minced red onion
    ½ cup seeded and diced
      cucumber
    ½ cup grated part-skim
      mozzarella cheese
    ½ cup Fresh Salsa (see page 23)

1. Preheat oven to 400° F. In a bowl mix tofu with cumin, cilantro, chili powder, salt substitute, and pepper.

2. In oil in a skillet over medium heat, brown tofu mixture lightly for 10 minutes. Let cool.

3. Using scissors, cut tortillas into wedges; bake until crisp (about 15 minutes) to make corn chips.

4. Place lettuce in a large salad bowl and spoon tofu mixture into the center of the leaves.

5. Arrange tomatoes, onion, and cucumber on top, and then sprinkle them with cheese and salsa. Serve slightly chilled.

Serves 6.

Note You can also place the tofu mixture in heatproof bowls, top with cheese, and broil until cheese melts just slightly. Then remove from oven and add to remaining ingredients.

Calories per serving: 217
Preparation time: 20 minutes
Cooking time: 20 minutes

There's nothing as refreshing in the heat of summer as Audrey's Spinach Salad, which features spinach leaves tossed with apples, currants, and red onion rings and dressed with a light curry sauce.

LIGHT AND EASY SALADS

In most European countries, preparing salads is not as complicated as in America. A salad bowl is filled with crisp butter lettuce and perhaps some curly endive, and then drizzled with vinegar, oil, salt, and pepper. This standard is served after the main course at every meal. The idea—which is exemplified by the following light, international salads—is to refresh and clear the palate, introduce some crispness of texture, and help stimulate the digestion with enzymes from green vegetables.

SPINACH AND PINE NUT SALAD

A variation on the spinach salad theme, this salad served with a Greek moussaka or a low-calorie lasagne makes a wonderful meal—the crunchiness of the salad complements the soft texture of eggplant or pasta. Prepare just before serving time for best flavor.

2 *bunches fresh spinach, washed and stemmed*
1 *red onion, sliced thinly*
½ *cup grated carrot*
½ *cup toasted pine nuts*
¼ *cup Greek Kalamata olives, pitted*
1 *cup crumbled part-skim feta cheese*
1 *tablespoon olive oil*
1 *tablespoon safflower oil*
1 *tablespoon wine vinegar*
1 *teaspoon lemon juice*
1 *teaspoon Dijon mustard*
 Herbal salt substitute and pepper, to taste

1. In a large salad bowl, mix spinach leaves, onion, carrot, nuts, olives, and feta cheese.

2. In another bowl, whisk together the dressing ingredients—oils, vinegar, lemon juice, mustard, salt substitute, and pepper. Pour over salad and toss. Serve immediately.

Serves 4 to 6.

Calories per serving: 376
Preparation time: 25 minutes

LOW-CALORIE TABBOULEH

Tabbouleh (pronounced tab-BOO-lee) is a festive salad from Lebanon. Although it has many recipe variations, its standard ingredients usually include mint, parsley, olive oil, and lemon juice. In this low-calorie version, colorful shredded vegetables are also added and olive oil is kept to a minimum. Tabbouleh keeps for up to five days if tightly covered and refrigerated.

2 *cups bulgur*
3 *cups boiling water*
2 *cups shredded red or green cabbage*
½ *large carrot, grated*
½ *cucumber, peeled and diced*
1 *stalk celery, chopped*
½ *cup chopped fresh mint*
2 *ripe tomatoes, chopped*
¾ *cup chopped green onions, including greens*
¼ *cup freshly squeezed lemon juice*
3½ *tablespoons olive oil*
2 *teaspoons herbal salt substitute*
1 *cup chopped parsley*
1 *small lemon, sliced, for garnish*

1. In a bowl place bulgur and boiling water and cover with a plate. Let sit for 20 minutes.

2. Mix cooked bulgur with remaining ingredients except lemon slices and chill for 1 hour. Serve cold with slices of lemon.

Serves 6.

Calories per serving: 301
Preparation time: 20 minutes
Cooking time: 20 minutes
Chilling time: 1 hour

INDONESIAN PEANUT SLAW

Made with blended tofu, this is a delicious salad with a traditional Asian dressing. Be sure to buy the soft variety of tofu to assure that the dressing is smooth.

4 *cups thinly sliced green cabbage (core removed)*
1 *cup grated carrot*
1 *cup chopped fresh pineapple*
2 *tablespoons peanuts, chopped*
1 *tablespoon currants*
1 *teaspoon chopped cilantro*
1 *cup soft tofu*
2 *teaspoons light sesame oil or safflower oil*
3 *tablespoons rice vinegar*
1 *tablespoon frozen orange juice concentrate*
1 *tablespoon honey*
¼ *teaspoon freshly ground pepper*
2 *tablespoons grated onion*

1. In a large salad bowl, place cabbage, carrot, pineapple, peanuts, currants, and cilantro.

2. Mix tofu, oil, vinegar, juice concentrate, honey, pepper, and onion in a blender until smooth, then toss with cabbage mixture until well coated. Chill for 20 minutes, then serve.

Serves 4.

Calories per serving: 165
Preparation time: 25 minutes
Chilling time: 20 minutes

MARINATED SALADS

A cup of cooked beans, leftover spaghetti, sliced mushrooms, or sweet onions—by themselves they may be uninspiring, but paired with a lemon-herb marinade, they become a tasty salad. Marinating is a terrific way to add flavors to salads without adding dreaded calories.

MARINATED CHICK-PEA AND LIMA BEAN SALAD

A delicious solution to leftover cooked beans, this salad can be part of an antipasto platter (see Marinated Mushroom and Chick-pea Appetizer, page 16) or can accompany a light fish or chicken entrée. Marinating the beans overnight improves the flavor dramatically. It can be prepared up to three days before serving, if stored in a tightly covered container in the refrigerator.

  2 cups cooked chick-peas
  2 cups cooked jumbo lima beans
  2 stalks celery, minced
  1 small onion, minced
  2 tablespoons minced parsley
  2 cloves garlic, minced, or more
    to taste
  3 tablespoons olive oil
  ⅓ cup lemon juice
  3 tablespoons red wine vinegar
  ¼ cup capers, drained
  1 tablespoon herbal salt
    substitute
    Freshly ground pepper, to taste
    Lettuce leaves, for lining bowl
    Red onion, thinly sliced, for
    garnish

Mix all ingredients except lettuce and red onion and let marinate from 2 hours to overnight. Serve in a lettuce-lined bowl; garnish with red onion rings.

Serves 6.

Calories per serving: 225
Preparation time: 20 minutes
Marinating time: 2–3 hours

GERMAN-STYLE POTATO SALAD WITH MINCED ONIONS

This potato salad gets its flavor from marinating warm potatoes in white wine. Serve with a light beef or chicken dish for an easy dinner. The salad will keep in a tightly covered container in the refrigerator for about four days. To avoid discoloring the potatoes, add radishes just before serving.

  4 cups diced boiled red potatoes
    (unpeeled)
  ⅓ cup dry white wine
  ⅛ teaspoon caraway seed,
    crushed
  ¼ cup plain, nonfat yogurt
  2 teaspoons olive oil
  1 teaspoon herbal salt
    substitute, or to taste
  ½ teaspoon freshly ground
    pepper
  2 teaspoons low-calorie
    mayonnaise
  1 teaspoon lemon juice
  ½ cup thinly sliced radishes
  ½ cup minced parsley
  1 tablespoon chopped fresh dill
    or 1 teaspoon dried dill
  ½ cup chopped green onions or
    white onions

1. Combine potatoes, white wine, and caraway seed and let marinate for 1 hour.

2. Add remaining ingredients and let marinate another 30 minutes before serving either chilled or at room temperature.

Serves 6 to 8.

Calories per serving: 136
Preparation time: 20 minutes
Marinating time: 90 minutes

SALAD SECRETS

Washing Use only the freshest greens for your salad. Inspect the edges and stalks of lettuce leaves, spinach, and other greens as you wash them, checking for wilted or browned spots. Spin the greens dry in a salad spinner or press dry on paper towels.

Storing Washed and dried greens can be kept for up to five days in the refrigerator without losing freshness. Just drain well after washing and store in a salad spinner or wrapped in slightly dampened paper towels in plastic bags.

Enhancing color and flavor Add color to your salads with reds and oranges—such as grated carrots (sprinkle with lemon juice to prevent browning), sliced or diced red bell pepper, cherry tomatoes, and sweet cherry peppers. Contrast flavors by mixing in a little curly endive for bitterness, grated Parmesan cheese for saltiness, and raisins for sweetening.

Choosing a salad dressing Select a dressing that contrasts with the rest of the meal, to balance the taste buds. If the meal is spicy, with sharp and pungent qualities, choose a creamy, mild-tasting dressing. If a low-key entrée or a rich but savory soup is planned, you may want to experiment with a vinaigrette.

Adding special touches Sprouts are fun in salads. Buy mung bean sprouts (an ingredient in many Chinese dishes), alfalfa sprouts, clover sprouts, and, for a zing, radish sprouts.

Plating the salad For special occasions, *plate* the individual salads; this is a restaurant term meaning to set up each person's salad on a small, chilled plate before the meal. Arrange it carefully, as if it were a piece of art. It will be sure to stimulate the eye as well as the tastebuds and will elicit many *ooh's* and *aah's*.

1. In a salad bowl gently toss cabbage, carrot, green onion, and parsley.

2. Whisk remaining ingredients in another bowl and pour over cabbage mixture. Toss well and let stand 20 minutes before serving.

Serves 6.

Calories per serving: 128
Preparation time: 25 minutes
Marinating time: 20 minutes

FRENCH BEAN SALAD

This delicate, yet filling, salad is lovely to look at. Steam the green beans until their bright color emerges and then immediately toss them with the marinade to keep the color bright. You can either leave the beans whole or slice them into bite-sized pieces, cutting diagonally. This salad will keep well for three to four days, if covered and refrigerated.

- 1 pound green beans, steamed lightly
- 1 cup cooked navy beans (approximately ½ cup raw) Juice of 1 lemon
- 2 ounces toasted, slivered almonds
- 1 tablespoon chopped parsley
- ¼ cup diced red bell pepper
- ¼ cup olive oil
- ⅓ cup rice vinegar
- 2 tablespoons Dijon mustard Lettuce leaves, for lining bowl

1. Combine all ingredients except lettuce and toss well to coat beans thoroughly.

2. Let marinate at room temperature for 45 minutes. Arrange in lettuce-lined bowl and serve.

Serves 4 to 6.

Calories per serving: 210
Preparation time: 25 minutes
Marinating time: 45 minutes

Shreds of carrot, green onion strips, and red cabbage compose this colorful slaw. The dressing is Asian style: sesame oil, rice vinegar, and mustard. Serve with Lemon Chicken With Roasted Green Peppers (see page 73) and roasted red potatoes for an easy picnic supper.

RED CABBAGE COLESLAW

Low in calories, yet rich in nutrients, this salad is particularly colorful for a coleslaw. The red of the cabbage contrasts with the green parsley and orange carrots. It will retain its texture and taste for two days if covered and stored in the refrigerator.

- 3 cups thinly sliced or shredded red cabbage
- 2 cups grated carrot
- ¼ cup minced green onion
- ½ cup minced parsley
- ⅓ cup freshly squeezed lemon juice
- ¼ cup rice vinegar
- 1 teaspoon dark sesame oil
- 1 tablespoon frozen apple juice concentrate
- 2 tablespoons stone-ground mustard
- ½ cup plain, nonfat yogurt
- 3 tablespoons safflower oil
- 1 tablespoon celery seed
- 1 tablespoon poppy seed

SZECHWAN NOODLES

Asian flavors blended with the subtle texture of noodles creates a spicy pasta salad. The pasta in this recipe can be found in most health-food or Japanese stores. Szechwan Noodles tastes best when left to marinate for at least 45 minutes before serving, although it can be stored for up to 48 hours. Add the peanuts (a good source of protein) at the last minute so they hold their crunchy consistency.

- 12 ounces cooked Japanese udon noodles
- 2 tablespoons grated fresh ginger
- 5 ounces sliced water chestnuts
- 2 cups sliced mushrooms
- 2 tablespoons chopped peanuts
- ¼ cup dark sesame oil
- 5 cloves garlic, minced, or more to taste
- 6 green onions (including green part), minced
- 1 to 2 teaspoons cayenne pepper, or to taste
- ½ cup low-sodium tamari or soy sauce
- ½ teaspoon honey
  Lettuce leaves, for lining bowl (optional)

1. Place pasta in a bowl. Mix together remaining ingredients except lettuce and toss with pasta.

2. Let marinate for 45 minutes before serving. Serve in a lettuce-lined bowl, if desired.

Serves 8.

> *Calories per serving: 170*
> *Preparation time: 25 minutes*
> *Marinating time: 45 minutes*

MEXICAN BEAN SALAD

Here's an unusual and delicious salad, discovered while the author was finishing some leftover Mexican food. It should be topped with Fresh Salsa (see page 23) or bottled salsa, available in almost all supermarkets.

Legumes, which include such foods as lima and pinto beans, are a rich source of protein and essential minerals, such as potassium and phosphorous. They contain about half the calories of an equal amount of meat—and none of the saturated fat and cholesterol.

Cook the beans the day before making the salad and chill them overnight. This bean salad will keep for three days in a covered container in the refrigerator. Serve this red and white salad on a bed of green spinach or lettuce for a colorful side dish to grilled fish. As a chilled dish, it can also provide a refresher when served with hot spicy Mexican food.

- 4 cups cooked lima beans (approximately 3 cups raw)
- 1 cup cooked pinto beans (approximately ⅔ cup raw)
- 2 cups Fresh Salsa (see page 23)
- 2 cups chopped green leaf lettuce
- 2 tomatoes, chopped
- 3 tablespoons chopped cilantro

1. Toss lima and pinto beans with salsa and marinate for 4 hours.

2. Place lettuce and tomato in salad bowl and spoon on beans; top with cilantro. Serve chilled.

Serves 6.

> *Calories per serving: 225*
> *Preparation time: 10 minutes*
> *Marinating time: 4 hours*

SUMMER RICE SALAD

Adapted to low-calorie cooking from a Los Angeles restaurant recipe, this inviting salad is perfect for lunch on a warm summer day. Be sure to seed the tomato so that it does not make the rice soggy.

- 2 cups cooked short-grain brown rice
- ¼ cup minced green onion
- ¼ cup seeded and minced green bell pepper
- 2 tablespoons minced parsley, plus minced parsley for garnish
- ½ cup peeled and diced jicama
- ¼ cup minced celery
- 4 radishes, sliced
- ¼ cup low-calorie mayonnaise
- 1 teaspoon low-sodium tamari or soy sauce
- 1 tablespoon lemon juice
- ¼ teaspoon cayenne pepper
- 1 tablespoon dry white wine
- 1 small tomato, seeded and cut into strips
  Red bell pepper, seeded and cut into rings, for garnish

Combine all ingredients except garnishes and toss well. Chill before serving. Garnish with red pepper rings and minced parsley.

Serves 4.

Note The tamari or soy sauce used in this recipe helps cut down on sodium—linked recently to high blood pressure by scientific studies.

> *Calories per serving: 193*
> *Preparation time: 25 minutes*
> *Chilling time: 30 minutes*

FRESH FRUIT SALADS

One welcome sight of approaching summer is the wide variety of fresh fruit appearing in the markets. Suddenly there are so many kinds of fruit; not just apples, bananas, and pears, but also peaches, plums, grapes, apricots, and berries. Following is a selection of easy, low-calorie recipes that make the most of fresh fruit flavors whether it's winter, spring, summer, or fall.

FIG AND YOGURT SALAD

This exotic sweet-tart combination is an excellent accompaniment for curries or Middle-Eastern foods. It can also be served like a chutney, with meats or chicken.

   *2 cups dried white figs
      (Calimyrna), stems removed,
      chopped*
   *⅓ cup dry white wine or
      port wine*
   *1 green apple (unpeeled), cored,
      stemmed, and grated*
   *1 small navel orange, peeled
      and chopped*
   ¼ cup diced celery
   ½ cup plain, nonfat yogurt
   ⅛ teaspoon turmeric
   ⅛ teaspoon ground cardamom
   *¼ teaspoon curry powder
      Lettuce leaves, for lining
      platter (optional)*

Mix figs and wine and let stand for 2 hours at room temperature. Then combine with other ingredients and serve, chilled or lukewarm, on a bed of lettuce, if used.

Serves 4.

Calories per serving: 317
Preparation time: 15 minutes
Marinating time: 2 hours

GREEN APPLE SALAD

Here's a tart low-calorie version of the traditional Waldorf salad. It is a crunchy salad chilled in a tangy marinade and focused on fresh autumn produce. The low-calorie mayonnaise, which contains only 40 calories per tablespoon compared to 80 to 100 found in regular mayonnaise, can be found in the diet section of most supermarkets and health-food stores. Prepare this dish within 2 hours of serving to keep it fresh.

   *5 cups diced green apples
      (unpeeled), cored and
      stemmed (see Note)*
   1 cup halved seedless red grapes
   1½ cups plain, nonfat yogurt
   *2 teaspoons low-calorie
      mayonnaise*
   1 teaspoon curry powder
   ½ cup currants
   ¼ cup diced celery
   ¼ teaspoon celery seed
   *1 tablespoon frozen apple juice
      concentrate*
   *1 teaspoon lemon juice
      Herbal salt substitute and
      pepper, to taste
      Lettuce leaves, for lining bowl*

Combine all ingredients and season to taste. Serve slightly chilled, on a bed of lettuce.

Serves 4.

Note To prevent apples from oxidizing (turning brown), you can place apple slices in a bowl of ice water mixed with lemon juice as you prepare them.

Calories per serving: 226
Preparation time: 20 minutes
Chilling time: 30 minutes

WATERCRESS AND GRAPEFRUIT ASPIC

Aspics are a beautiful way to present fresh fruits and vegetables: in a shimmering, lightly tinted gelatin. The delicate colors of watercress and pale fruits make this a perfect springtime salad that goes well with light fish dishes. You can prepare it up to a day in advance, but don't remove the mold until right before serving.

   *1 envelope unflavored gelatin or
      2 teaspoons agar flakes*
   ½ cup apple juice
   *¼ cup freshly squeezed
      lemon juice*
   *1 cup chilled grapefruit juice,
      preferably fresh*
   *½ teaspoon safflower oil,
      for mold*
   1 cup peeled grapefruit sections
   *1 cup shredded watercress, plus
      watercress for garnish
      Lettuce leaves, for lining
      platter*

1. In a small saucepan combine gelatin (or agar flakes) and apple juice; simmer until gelatin (or agar flakes) dissolves. Add lemon and grapefruit juices and stir well.

2. Pour into a 9- by 12-inch glass baking dish and chill until gelatin begins to set.

3. Lightly oil dessert mold. Stir the grapefruit and watercress into the partially set gelatin and spoon into the prepared mold. Chill until completely set (about 1¼ hours).

4. To remove the mold, turn it on edge and tap gently, or run the bottom under hot water for a few seconds. Turn aspic onto lettuce-lined platter and garnish with additional watercress.

Serves 4.

Calories per serving: 72
Preparation time: 10 minutes
Chilling time: 75 minutes

MOLDED FRUIT SALAD

Another delicious aspic, this salad is molded in a grape-juice mixture. Use purple grape juice for an informal, festive salad, or white grape juice for a more formal occasion. You can also experiment with some of the newly released nonalcoholic wines—they taste like wine but are made of unfermented varietal grape juices and work well in this recipe.

    3   cups grape juice or
        nonalcoholic wine
    1   packet unflavored gelatin or
        2 teaspoons agar flakes (sea-
        weed gelatin)
    1½ cups halved seedless black or
        red grapes
    1   cup peeled and seeded
        tangerine sections (see Note)
    1   cup halved seedless
        green grapes
    ½   teaspoon safflower oil,
        for mold
        Lettuce leaves, for lining
        platter

1. In a large saucepan, simmer grape juice with gelatin until it is dissolved. Pour mixture into a 9- by 12-inch glass baking dish and let partially congeal in refrigerator.

2. Mix black grapes, tangerine sections, and green grapes; add to the partially congealed gelatin. Lightly oil a decorative mold or soufflé dish. Pour gelatin into mold and let chill until completely set (about 1¼ hours).

3. To remove the mold, turn it on its edge and tap gently, or run the bottom under hot water for a few seconds. Turn Molded Fruit Salad onto a lettuce-lined platter and serve.

Serves 6.

<u>Note</u> If tangerines are unavailable, seeded orange sections may be used.

Calories per serving: 149
Preparation time: 15 minutes
Chilling time: 75 minutes

Almost a sculpture, this delicate Molded Fruit Salad can be made with white grape juice and slices of fresh tangerines and red and green grapes. Serve with iced mint tea.

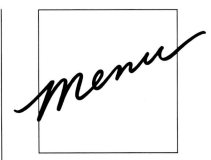

MAKE-AHEAD DINNER FOR SIX

Jicama and Citrus Salad

Roast Lamb Breton-Style

Broiled Tomato Halves

Steamed Broccoli

Lemon Strawberry Mousse

*Assortment of Sparkling Waters
With Lemon Slices*

This menu has the advantage of many make-ahead elements: The salad can be prepared in the morning and chilled during the day; the broccoli can be washed and trimmed and the tomatoes can be halved the same morning; the lamb can be roasted and beans baked the night before; and the mousse can be whipped and spooned into individual dessert glasses hours before the guests arrive. Broil the tomatoes cut side up for 3 to 4 minutes just before serving. Leftover lamb can be made into stew or sliced for a marinated salad for lunch the next day. All recipes serve six.

JICAMA AND CITRUS SALAD

This colorful salad combines the Mexican vegetable jicama with fresh orange and grapefruit.

    2   cups peeled and julienned
        jicama
    1   red bell pepper, seeded and
        cut into thin strips
    1   cup peeled orange sections
    ½   cup peeled grapefruit sections
        (remove as much white
        membrane as possible with
        a serrated knife)
    2   tablespoons chopped
        fresh mint
    2   tablespoons frozen orange
        juice concentrate
        Juice of 2 oranges
    1   tablespoon lemon juice
    ¼   teaspoon minced garlic
        Watercress or romaine lettuce,
        shredded, for lining bowl

Mix all ingredients and spoon over watercress in a decorative salad bowl. Cover with plastic wrap and chill for 30 minutes. Serve chilled.

Serves 6.

Calories per serving: 68
Preparation time: 25 minutes
Chilling time: 30 minutes

ROAST LAMB BRETON-STYLE

In Brittany this main course is traditionally served in springtime.

    1   small leg of lamb (about
        3 lb)
        Herbal salt substitute and
        pepper, to taste
    4   cloves garlic, sliced thinly
    2   cups dried white beans (such
        as navy or lima beans)
    2   cups chopped onion
    2   bay leaves, crushed
    2   cups chopped tomato
    1   teaspoon butter

1. Preheat oven to 325° F. Rub leg of lamb well with salt substitute and pepper. With a knife point, pierce small holes in lamb and insert slices of garlic throughout. Place lamb in a roasting pan and cook until pink and juicy in the center and browned on the outside (about 2 hours).

2. While the lamb roasts, bring 5 cups of water to a boil and cook dried beans with onion, bay leaves, tomato, and butter. Boil for 40 minutes, then add more water if needed, cover, and cook over medium heat until soft (about 1 hour longer). Remove bay leaves.

3. Transfer beans to baking dish. Add several spoonfuls of juice from roasting lamb to beans, place in the 325° F oven and bake for 15 minutes. To serve, slice roasted lamb and accompany with beans.

Serves 6 to 8.

Calories per serving: 460
Preparation time: 10 minutes
Cooking time: 2 hours

LEMON STRAWBERRY MOUSSE

A delightful, light dessert, this mousse is also a beautiful bright pink from the puréed strawberries.

    ½   cup puréed fresh strawberries
    3   tablespoons arrowroot powder
    ½   cup freshly squeezed lemon
        juice
    3   tablespoons honey
    ¼   teaspoon vanilla
    1   egg yolk, lightly beaten
    6   egg whites
        Sliced strawberries and grated
        lemon rind, for garnish

1. In a saucepan over medium heat place strawberries, arrowroot, lemon juice, honey, vanilla, and egg yolk, stirring, until mixture thickens to a custard consistency (3 to 5 minutes). Immediately pour into a clean bowl and chill.

2. Whip egg whites until stiff peaks form. Gently fold into chilled custard and spoon mousse into 6 dessert dishes or wineglasses. Chill for 1 hour, then garnish with sliced strawberries and grated lemon rind and serve.

Serves 6.

Calories per serving: 91
Preparation time: 20 minutes
Chilling time: 1 hour

This make-ahead menu features Roast Lamb Breton-Style, a light citrus and jicama salad, and lemon and strawberries whipped into a creamy mousse.

To capture the finest flavors without heavy salt, base vegetable entrées on farm-fresh produce. Vegetable dishes are ideal for elegant low-calorie cooking.

Vegetable Dishes

Supplementing your menus with a few vegetarian recipes is one easy way to avoid the heavy calories that accompany meat-based meals. These dishes are not just for vegetarians; they are delicious enough to satisfy guests who usually prefer meat dishes. You'll find exotic recipes, such as Curried Vegetables With Raita and Chutney (see page 58), as well as more traditional dishes: Broccoli-Ricotta Soufflé (see page 63), Ratatouille Crêpes (see page 62), and Vegetarian Sushi Rolls (see page 64). In addition step-by-step instructions are provided for making crêpes (see page 61) and casseroles (see page 60). Finally, a French candlelight dinner (see page 67) will banish the thought that vegetarian food is boring.

DOWN-HOME DINNERS

These family-style recipes are designed to please a crowd of hearty eaters but are also amazingly low in calories. Most can be made ahead—a boon to the busy cook.

BARLEY-STUFFED CABBAGE ROLLS WITH GINGER SAUCE

This delicious recipe is from a cook named Susan, who specializes in macrobiotic cookery from Japan. She uses the salty flavor of *hijiki*, a common Japanese seaweed used for seasoning, to bring out the sweetness of the green cabbage. You can prepare these rolls ahead of time and refrigerate them for up to 24 hours before baking.

- 1 head green cabbage
- 3 tablespoons dried hijiki, rinsed well in running water
- 5 dried black Japanese mushrooms
- 1 cup boiling water
- 2 teaspoons dark sesame oil
- 1 onion, sliced thinly
- ½ cup shredded carrot
- ½ cup shredded celery
- 1 cup cooked brown rice
- 1 tablespoon nutritional yeast (yellow flakes)
  Low-sodium tamari or soy sauce, to taste
  Safflower oil, for greasing baking dish

Ginger Sauce

- 1 cup cashews
- 2 cups cold water
- 1 teaspoon safflower oil
- 2 tablespoons fresh ginger, grated
- 2 tablespoons whole wheat pastry flour
- ¼ teaspoon white pepper
  Pinch cayenne pepper
- 1 teaspoon low-sodium tamari or soy sauce

1. Preheat oven to 350° F. With a sharp knife, core center of cabbage head, leaving head intact. Place cabbage in a large pot and fill with 3 to 4 inches of water. Steam until leaves are tender enough to peel off easily

and fold without breaking (about 20 minutes). Drain cabbage and set aside. While cabbage is cooking, place hijiki and mushrooms in a small bowl with the boiling water and steep.

2. In a wok or skillet, heat 1 teaspoon of the sesame oil and sauté onion until soft but not browned. Add carrot and celery and cook, stirring, for several minutes more. Add rice, nutritional yeast, and tamari, if needed. Remove from heat.

3. Drain hijiki and mushrooms. Slice stems off mushrooms and chop caps coarsely. Add caps and hijiki to rice mixture.

4. Separate leaves of cabbage. Lightly grease a 9- by 12-inch shallow baking dish.

5. Wrap reserved cabbage leaves around rice mixture by placing 1 to 2 tablespoons of filling on the bottom section of each leaf, folding sides in, and rolling up like a sleeping bag.

6. Place cabbage rolls, seam side down, in baking dish. Lightly brush with remaining 1 teaspoon sesame oil. Bake cabbage rolls for 45 minutes.

Serves 6.

Ginger Sauce

1. In a blender combine cashews with the water and purée. Strain through a sieve into a bowl.

2. In a saucepan heat safflower oil and sauté ginger for 1 minute, then add flour. Cook over low heat, stirring, for 2 minutes to eliminate floury taste. Slowly pour in cashew milk, stirring with a whisk as you pour. Mixture should thicken. Season with white pepper, cayenne, and tamari and serve with cabbage rolls.

> *Calories per serving: 251*
> *Preparation time: 40–50 minutes*
> *Cooking time: 45 minutes*

BLACK BEAN CHILI WITH CILANTRO

A favorite dish at Greens at Fort Mason restaurant in San Francisco, this southwestern chili has been influenced by South American cuisine. Black beans are savory and hold their shape while cooking. In this recipe they are blended with cilantro, grated onion, and low-calorie cheese for a meal in one dish.

- ¼ cup dry sherry
- 1 tablespoon olive oil
- 2 cups chopped onion
- ½ cup chopped celery
- ½ cup chopped carrot
- ½ cup seeded and chopped red bell pepper
- 4 cups cooked black beans (approximately 3½ cups raw)
- 2 cups Vegetarian Stock (see page 31) or water
- 2 tablespoons minced garlic
- 1 cup chopped tomatoes
- 2 teaspoons ground cumin
- 4 teaspoons chili powder, or to taste
- ½ teaspoon oregano
- ¼ cup chopped cilantro
- 2 tablespoons honey
- 2 tablespoons tomato paste
  Yogurt, grated onion, and grated low-calorie Monterey jack cheese, for garnish

1. In a large, heavy pot, heat sherry and oil and sauté onions until soft but not browned.

2. Add celery, carrot, and bell pepper and sauté 5 minutes, stirring frequently.

3. Add remaining ingredients except garnishes and bring to a boil. Lower heat and simmer for 45 minutes to 1 hour, covered. Chili should be thick with all water absorbed. Garnish with grated onion, cheese, and a dollop of yogurt.

Serves 6 to 8.

> *Calories per serving: 196*
> *Preparation time: 35 minutes*
> *Cooking time: 45–60 minutes*

TEX-MEX CHILI

This recipe combines the traditional Texas chili spices of cumin and hot peppers with the tangy cilantro of Mexican cuisine. Tex-Mex Chili can be easily made ahead and refrigerated for a week.

- 2 *large onions, chopped*
- ¼ *cup Vegetarian Stock (see page 31) or white wine*
- 3 *cloves garlic, minced*
- 1 *bell pepper, chopped*
- 2 *teaspoons chili powder, or to taste*
- 2 *teaspoons ground oregano*
- 1 *teaspoon ground cumin*
- 4 *cups cooked kidney or pinto beans (approximately 3 cups raw)*
- 2 *cups water or vegetable broth*
- 1 *cup rich tomato sauce*
- 2 *tablespoons chopped cilantro plus chopped cilantro, for garnish*
  Plain, nonfat yogurt, for garnish

1. In a heavy Dutch oven or stockpot, sauté onion in vegetable stock until onion is soft, then add garlic, bell pepper, chili powder, oregano, cumin, 3 cups of the beans, and the water. Bring to a boil.

2. In a blender purée the remaining 1 cup beans with tomato sauce. Add this mixture to the chili with the 2 tablespoons cilantro.

3. Cook chili in stockpot over low to medium heat for 20 minutes, covered. Chili can also be slow-cooked in an electric slow cooker on low, for 6 to 8 hours. Stir occasionally. Serve hot, garnished with cilantro and yogurt.

Serves 6 to 8.

<u>Note</u> Chili improves in flavor if allowed to sit overnight in the refrigerator. It can also be frozen for up to two months.

Calories per serving: 148
Preparation time: 20 minutes
Cooking time: 35 minutes

Velvety black beans are simmered with cumin, garlic, cilantro, and sherry to make a rich Black Bean Chili With Cilantro that rivals the best of the Southwest, with half the calories. Serve with corn-bread sticks and a small green salad.

REPLACING SALT WITH HERBS AND SPICES

The more salt you eat, the more water you retain to dilute it. You don't want the extra water weight, of course, and it may also hide a loss of body fat, depriving you of your reward when you step on the scale. Also, research has linked excessive salt intake to hypertension and heart and kidney disease. Using herbs and spices is a way to get the full flavors from food without adding a lot of salt.

First experiment with some of the more basic herbs and spices. Remember, when cooking with herbs, the longer herbs sit after the dish has been cooked the more flavorful they become. Also, many herbs actually fare better under brief cooking conditions. For example, dill and basil lose their flavor, and sage, rosemary, and thyme become very pungent and bitter when subject to prolonged cooking.

Spices are often sweeter if roasted first. If you have the time, simply roast them over medium heat in an ungreased skillet until you smell a nutlike aroma.

Here's a list of dried and fresh herbs, spices, and flavorings that work well in different dishes.
Beans: bay leaf, chili powder, coriander, cumin, mustard
Fruit desserts: cinnamon, cloves, mint, mace, nutmeg
Grains: curry powder, marjoram, parsley, thyme
Fresh green beans: dill, dried lemon peel, summer savory
Potatoes: chives, oregano, paprika, parsley, rosemary, tarragon
Salad dressings (such as vinaigrettes): fresh or dried basil, celery seed, chervil, fresh dill, parsley
Soup stock: bay leaf, fresh or dried basil, marjoram, fresh parsley, thyme
Tomato salad: fresh or dried basil, celery seed, fresh dill, garlic, tarragon
Tomato sauces: chervil, garlic, marjoram, oregano, fresh parsley, sage, summer savory

STUFFED SWEET RED BELL PEPPERS

Try this recipe when sweet red bell peppers are in season. Choose well-shaped peppers that, when stuffed, can stand up in a dish. The light filling and sauce can be made ahead, and even frozen. Prepare the peppers right before baking, however, because they will lose their color and flavor if allowed to sit too long.

    4 medium-sized red bell peppers
    1 teaspoon sesame oil
    1 onion, chopped finely
    2 cups sliced mushrooms
    1 teaspoon minced garlic
    1 cup corn (frozen or fresh)
    2 eggs, beaten
    1 cup grated farmer cheese
    2 tablespoons grated Parmesan
       cheese

1. Preheat oven to 350° F. Heat a saucepan of water to boiling. Cut tops off bell peppers. Remove ribs and seeds. Chop tops and reserve. Immerse scooped-out bell peppers in boiling water for 2 minutes to soften, then rinse under cold water. Set aside to stuff later.

2. In a skillet heat oil and sauté onion until soft, then add mushrooms and garlic and cook until mushrooms begin to weep moisture.

3. Add chopped pepper tops and corn to skillet. Sauté, stirring frequently, for 3 minutes, then add eggs and farmer and Parmesan cheeses and turn off heat.

4. Place peppers in a deep baking dish and stuff with sautéed filling. Cover with foil and bake until bubbling, lightly browned, and soft (about 45 minutes). Serve hot.

Serves 4.

> *Calories per serving: 219*
> *Preparation time: 35 minutes*
> *Baking time: 45 minutes*

EGGPLANT AND CHICK-PEA MOUSSAKA

Greek cooks traditionally salt eggplant before baking, to allow the fibers to soften and therefore better absorb the flavors of the sauce. The salt can be rinsed off before cooking. This savory dish will freeze well and keeps for seven days covered tightly with plastic wrap in the refrigerator. It is a nice low-calorie twist on the traditional beef moussaka.

    1   large eggplant, sliced
         very thinly
         Salt
    1   tablespoon olive oil
    1   large onion, sliced
    2   cloves garlic, minced
    2   large ripe tomatoes, chopped
    3   tablespoons chopped fresh
         basil
    1   to 2 teaspoons dried oregano
    ½   cup white wine
         Oil, for greasing pan
    1   cup cooked chick-peas
    2   eggs, beaten lightly
    2   tablespoons grated Parmesan
         cheese

1. Preheat oven to 300° F. Place eggplant slices on a large baking tray (use two trays if needed) and lightly sprinkle with salt. Bake until easily pierced with a fork (10 to 15 minutes).

2. While eggplant is baking, heat olive oil in a skillet and sauté onion until soft, then add garlic, tomatoes, basil, oregano, and wine. Continue to sauté until tomatoes soften (about 10 minutes).

3. Rinse eggplant, if desired, and place in a lightly greased 9- by 12-inch baking dish. Raise temperature of oven to 350° F.

4. Spread chick-peas over eggplant; top with beaten eggs. Spoon tomato sauté over eggs. Sprinkle with cheese and bake for 45 minutes. Serve hot.

Serves 4 to 6.

> *Calories per serving: 143*
> *Preparation time: 35 minutes*
> *Cooking time: 45 minutes*

MEDITERRANEAN STUFFED EGGPLANT

Eggplant and zucchini are ideal for stuffing and baking. You can then serve them as entrées or side dishes. This Mediterranean-style stuffed eggplant carries the flavors of tomato, garlic, olive oil, and peppers. Steam, bake, or blanch the eggplant before using so that the texture is as soft as the filling. This vegetable dish will keep two days in the refrigerator before baking if tightly covered with plastic wrap.

> 2 medium-sized eggplants
> 2 teaspoons olive oil, plus oil for greasing pan
> ¼ cup dry sherry
> ½ cup chopped onion
> 3 to 4 cloves garlic, minced
> 1 cup coarsely chopped plum tomatoes
> 1 green onion (including greens), chopped
> ½ cup seeded and chopped bell pepper
> ¼ cup black olives, chopped
> 1 teaspoon minced fresh basil
> ½ teaspoon oregano
> Herbal salt substitute and freshly ground pepper, to taste
> ½ to ¾ cup whole wheat bread crumbs, plus finely ground whole wheat bread crumbs, for topping
> ⅓ cup grated Parmesan cheese
> Chopped fresh basil or parsley, for garnish

1. Preheat oven to 350° F. Slice eggplants in half lengthwise. Place eggplant, cut side down, on an aluminum-foil–lined baking sheet. Brush outside of eggplant with olive oil. Bake until a knife inserted into skin pierces easily (about 20 minutes), then remove from oven and let cool.

2. With a sharp-edged spoon, scoop out the insides of the eggplants into a bowl. Place the eggplant shells in a lightly greased baking dish, wedging them together so they stay upright.

3. In a skillet heat sherry and sauté onion until onion is soft but not browned. Add garlic, tomatoes, green onion, bell pepper, olives, basil, oregano, and salt substitute and pepper and sauté for 5 minutes, stirring frequently.

4. Remove from heat and stir in bread crumbs and Parmesan cheese, adding enough bread crumbs to form a thick filling.

5. Stuff filling into eggplant shells and top with finely ground bread crumbs. Season, if desired, with salt substitute and pepper.

6. Bake stuffed eggplants until browned and bubbling (about 25 minutes). Serve hot, garnished with basil.

Serves 4.

Calories per serving: 207
Preparation time: 35 minutes
Baking time: 45 minutes

Eggplant is softened by baking, then spread with tomatoes, onions, chickpeas, cheese, and pungent spices, and baked again. Serve Eggplant and Chickpea Moussaka crisp and hot; it makes hearty fare for chilly weather.

CURRIED VEGETABLES WITH RAITA AND CHUTNEY

In the marketplaces of Indian cities and towns, the vendors squat beside round baskets of shimmering spices. Translated into American cooking terms, these spices mean *curry*, which is a mixture of 5 to 12 spices, made hot or mild according to the combination. Here is a medium-hot curried vegetable dish, accompanied by a cooling Cucumber Raita (pronounced RIGHT-ah) and a sweet chutney. The curried vegetables and chutney freeze well, but serve the raita within 24 hours of making it, for best flavor.

- 2 tablespoons turmeric
- 1 tablespoon cumin seed, ground
- 2 teaspoons freshly ground black pepper
- 1 teaspoon cayenne pepper
- 2 tablespoons coriander seed, ground
- 1 tablespoon caraway seed, ground
- 2 tablespoons cinnamon
- 1 tablespoon grated fresh ginger
- 2 tablespoons ground cardamom
- 1 teaspoon safflower oil
- ½ cup dry sherry
- 2 cups sliced onions
- 4 cups peeled and cubed eggplant
- 1 cup sliced carrot rounds
- 1 small russet or red potato, cubed
- 2 cups thinly sliced mushrooms
- 1 tablespoon minced garlic
- 2 cups apple juice
- ¼ cup freshly squeezed lemon juice

Cucumber Raita

- 2 teaspoons whole cumin seed
- 1 teaspoon herbal salt substitute
- 1 large cucumber, peeled, seeded, and coarsely grated
- ½ small apple (unpeeled), cored and coarsely grated
- ⅛ teaspoon cayenne pepper
- 1½ cups plain, nonfat yogurt

Ginger-Apple Chutney

- 3 cooking apples (unpeeled), cored and chopped
- 3 ripe pears (unpeeled), cored and chopped
- 1 clove garlic, minced
- 2 tablespoons grated fresh ginger
- ½ cup orange juice
- ½ cup apple juice
- 1 teaspoon cinnamon
- 1 teaspoon ground cloves
- 1 teaspoon herbal salt substitute
- ¼ cup apple cider vinegar
- ¼ cup honey
  Dash of cayenne pepper

1. In a large skillet place turmeric, cumin seed, black pepper, cayenne, coriander seed, caraway seed, cinnamon, ginger, and cardamom. Roast over low heat, stirring frequently, until an aroma emerges from the mixture (about 5 minutes).

2. Add oil, sherry, and onions, and cook over medium heat until onions are soft but not browned (8 to 10 minutes).

3. Add eggplant, carrot, potato, mushrooms, garlic, apple juice, and lemon juice. Bring to a boil, then lower heat to simmer and cook 15 to 20 minutes. Serve hot.

Serves 6.

Cucumber Raita

1. In an ungreased skillet roast cumin and salt substitute over low heat until aroma emerges (about 5 minutes).

2. Grind cumin and salt substitute in a blender or spice mill. In a bowl combine with remaining ingredients and chill until serving time.

Makes 3 cups.

Ginger-Apple Chutney

1. In a saucepan bring all ingredients to a boil, and cook over medium-high heat for 30 minutes.

2. Mash with a potato masher, or purée lightly in blender. Serve warm or cold.

Makes 3 cups.

Calories per serving: 406
Preparation time: 55 minutes
Cooking time: 55 minutes

BAKED TOFU

These tofu cutlets are well seasoned with a spice mixture. Try them in sandwiches or as a light entrée with a mushroom gravy or baked in a tomato-cheese sauce.

- 1 pound firm tofu, drained
- 3 tablespoons whole wheat flour
- 2 tablespoons nutritional yeast (yellow flakes)
- 1 tablespoon minced garlic
- 1 tablespoon onion powder
- ¼ teaspoon ground oregano
- 1 teaspoon poultry seasoning
- 1 teaspoon low-sodium tamari or soy sauce
- 1 teaspoon dark sesame oil
  Oil, for greasing pan

1. Preheat oven to 350° F. Slice tofu into eight equal-sized slabs. Place them on a paper-towel-lined baking sheet; cover with another single layer of paper towels and weight tofu with a phone book or a large cutting board for 30 minutes.

2. In a bowl mix together flour, yeast, garlic, onion powder, oregano, and poultry seasoning. In another bowl combine tamari and sesame oil.

3. Lightly grease a 9- by 12-inch baking sheet.

4. Coat tofu pieces with tamari mixture, then with flour mixture, covering all surfaces. Place on the baking sheet and cook, turning once, until both sides are lightly browned (15 to 25 minutes). Serve hot.

Serves 4.

Calories per serving: 125
Preparation time: 45 minutes
Baking time: 15–25 minutes

BAKED MACARONI PRIMAVERA

Primavera is a much-loved Italian springtime dish of pasta and vegetables in a light cream sauce. This low-calorie version combines whole wheat macaroni with a medley of fresh vegetables sautéed in sherry and olive oil, and is tossed with a light béchamel made from nonfat milk and a little Parmesan cheese. Make this casserole ahead and freeze it—it is elegant enough to serve to company, and easy enough for a busy weeknight dinner.

> 8 ounces dried whole wheat, spinach, or artichoke macaroni
> Oil, for greasing baking dish
> ¼ cup dry sherry
> 1 teaspoon olive oil
> ⅓ cup chopped green onion (including greens)
> 1 teaspoon minced garlic
> 1 red bell pepper, seeded and chopped
> ¼ teaspoon ground cumin
> ½ teaspoon dried oregano
> 1 tablespoon chopped fresh basil
> ½ cup asparagus, cut diagonally into 2-inch lengths
> 1 cup halved cherry tomatoes
> ½ cup whole snow peas, trimmed

Primavera Sauce

> 2 teaspoons butter or margarine
> 2 teaspoons flour
> 1 cup nonfat milk
> ⅓ cup grated Parmesan cheese
> ¼ teaspoon white pepper

1. Preheat oven to 400° F. In a large pot heat water to boil. Add pasta and, uncovered, cook until al dente (cooked but not mushy). Drain and rinse pasta under cold water. Place in a large bowl and set aside.

2. Lightly grease a large baking dish. In a skillet heat sherry and olive oil and sauté green onion, garlic, and bell pepper until pepper is soft but not mushy. Add cumin, oregano, basil, asparagus, cherry tomatoes, and snow peas, and sauté 2 minutes, stirring frequently.

3. Remove from heat and toss with pasta and Primavera Sauce. Spoon into baking dish. Bake until lightly browned and bubbling (about 25 minutes).

Serves 4 to 6.

Primavera Sauce In a saucepan heat butter and stir in flour. Cook 2 minutes, stirring, to eliminate floury taste, then slowly add milk, stirring with a whisk. If milk is added slowly enough, the sauce should thicken to a heavy cream consistency. Add cheese and pepper.

Calories per serving: 225
Preparation time: 45 minutes
Baking time: 25 minutes

The bright colors of fresh vegetables join wheat macaroni in a light cheese sauce. Baked Macaroni Primavera is an elegant springtime dish served with tossed green salad and a fruit dessert.

 *Basics*

CASSEROLE BUILDING

Vegetable casseroles are both easy to make and easy to make ahead. They are the busy dieter's most dependable main course. Here are a few easy tips to make your casseroles moist and flavorful. You will need the following.

Base such as sautéed vegetables, a cooked grain or bean, tofu

Liquid such as stock, nonfat milk, wine, water

Binder such as beaten egg, low-fat cheeses, bread crumbs

Flavoring such as herbs, spices, low-fat cheeses, onions, garlic

Casseroles are usually baked in a moderate (350° F) oven until they are set (about 40 minutes). You may want to cover the casserole with aluminum foil to allow the interior to cook faster, but remember to remove the foil during the last 15 minutes in order to lightly brown the top.

1. Start with an assortment of vegetables and sauté them in a very small amount of oil (less than 1 teaspoon), plus a little dry sherry or water. By sautéing them first, you'll get much more flavor in the casserole.

2. Then add the protein source, usually cooked grains (such as rice), beans (such as cooked pinto beans or chick-peas), or tofu. Mix everything together.

3. Now take the casserole dish and begin building. Fill the dish with the above mixture to about three fourths of the way to the top. Pour in wine or broth, about ¼ cup, just to keep everything from drying out as the casserole cooks.

4. To bind the casserole, add beaten egg, small amounts of grated low-fat cheeses, or bread crumbs. Pour binder over the casserole or sprinkle on top. As the casserole bakes, these ingredients will help to solidify the mixture.

EASY FOR ENTERTAINING

Ever wonder what to serve to those health-conscious friends who are trying to cut back on meat? Now you can choose one of the following vegetarian recipes from around the world and serve it with pride.

TOFU TERIYAKI

Here's a great combination—sweet-and-sour vegetables and tofu—that you can prepare ahead of time, and keep in a tightly covered container in the refrigerator for up to four days before serving.

- *1 tablespoon sesame oil*
- *1 pound firm tofu, drained and cut into 1-inch cubes*
- *2 cups chopped vegetables (onion, red bell pepper, squash, and broccoli, or whatever you have available)*
- *2 tablespoons rice vinegar*
- *½ cup low-sodium tamari or soy sauce*
- *3 tablespoons honey*
- *⅓ cup sherry or mirin (Japanese sweet rice wine)*

1. In a skillet or wok heat oil and lightly sauté tofu until browned. It may fall apart a little, which is fine. When browned, remove tofu to a platter and set it aside.

2. Add a little more sesame oil to skillet, if needed, and sauté vegetables until tender.

3. In a small saucepan heat rice vinegar, tamari, honey, and sherry until boiling. Reduce heat and simmer sauce for 5 minutes.

4. Add tofu to vegetable sauté and pour sauce over all. Heat through and serve hot.

Serves 4.

> *Calories per serving: 224*
> *Preparation time: 20 minutes*
> *Cooking time: 15 minutes*

SPINACH AND CHEESE SOUFFLÉ ROLL

This is a scrumptious entrée: a layered spinach mixture with a soufflé-like texture, topped by mixed cheeses and rolled and sliced like a jelly roll. The French call it a roulade.

- *⅓ cup finely minced onion*
- *1 teaspoon olive oil*
- *3 cups washed and chopped fresh spinach leaves*
- *⅓ cup finely minced parsley*
- *¼ cup grated part-skim mozzarella cheese*
- *6 eggs, separated Safflower oil, for greasing parchment*
- *2 cups grated farmer cheese*
- *2 tablespoons grated Parmesan cheese*

1. Preheat oven to 400° F. In a medium skillet over medium-high heat, sauté onion in olive oil until onion is very soft. Add spinach and parsley and cover. Cook over low heat for 2 minutes. Drain if needed.

2. Transfer to a bowl. Stir mozzarella and egg yolks into spinach mixture.

3. Cut a piece of parchment paper to fit into a 9- by 12-inch shallow baking dish; lightly oil the parchment.

4. In a separate bowl beat egg whites until soft peaks form and fold them into spinach mixture. Spoon into the parchment-lined baking dish. Cover with another piece of lightly oiled parchment. Bake for 25 minutes.

5. In a small bowl mix farmer and Parmesan cheeses. When soufflé is baked, flip it out of the baking dish onto a counter. Peel off the top sheet of parchment and spread the cheese mixture over soufflé.

6. Roll soufflé and cheese mixture as you would a jelly roll, peeling off the second sheet of parchment as you go. Cut into thick slices and serve.

Serves 6.

> *Calories per serving: 229*
> *Preparation time: 20 minutes*
> *Baking time: 25 minutes*

MU SHU TOFU

A favorite, but calorie-rich Chinese dish is mu shu pork, a stir-fried pork mixture wrapped in small pancakes and dipped into a rich sauce. This low-calorie, vegetarian version uses a savory stir-fry of carrots, onions, and tofu and a spicy peanut sauce for dipping. The pancakes are easy to make, but you can cook just the stir-fry and serve it with the peanut sauce for a delicious dinner. The sauce keeps two weeks in the refrigerator and is good over chicken or fish, too.

> 1 teaspoon safflower oil
> 1 cup grated carrot
> 2 cups tofu, cut into small chunks
> 2 green onions, cut into diagonal slices
> 2 tablespoons grated fresh ginger
> 2 tablespoons dry sherry
> ½ teaspoon honey
> 2 tablespoons vegetable stock or water

Pancakes

> 2 cups white or whole wheat pastry flour
> ¾ cup boiling water (approximately)
> 2 teaspoons sesame oil

Peanut Sauce

> 2 tablespoons chunky peanut butter
> ¼ teaspoon cayenne pepper
> 1½ tablespoons honey
> 2 tablespoons low-sodium tamari or soy sauce
> 2 teaspoons rice vinegar
> 1 tablespoon minced green onion
> 1½ teaspoons ground coriander
> 2 teaspoons sesame oil

1. Prepare Pancakes. In a wok or skillet, heat safflower oil and sauté carrots and tofu for 3 minutes, stirring constantly. Add remaining ingredients and increase heat until the mixture begins to bubble.

2. Cook uncovered until most of the liquid has evaporated. While vegetables are cooking, prepare Peanut Sauce.

3. To assemble, each person places a few spoonfuls of filling on top of a pancake, adds sauce, and rolls pancake into a cylinder.

Serves 6.

Pancakes

1. In a large bowl mix flour and boiling water with a wooden spoon and turn onto a lightly floured surface. Knead together until an elastic dough forms that is soft, pliable, and not sticky.

2. On a floured surface roll out dough to about ¼-inch thickness; cut into 2½-inch rounds. Roll out each round to 5-inch-diameter pancake.

3. Lightly brush one side of each pancake with sesame oil. Place pairs of pancakes back-to-back, with oil in between them. (Oil keeps one side of pancake soft during cooking and later in wrapping and filling stages.)

4. Heat an ungreased skillet and cook each unoiled side of the pair of pancakes over low heat until slightly brown. Remove from skillet, peel apart and stack under a dampened dish towel until ready to use.

Makes 12 to 15 pancakes.

Peanut Sauce In a small bowl stir together all ingredients. Serve with pancakes and filling.

Makes ½ cup.

> *Calories per serving: 289*
> *Preparation time: 45 minutes*
> *Cooking time: 20 minutes*

Step-by-Step

HOW TO MAKE CRÊPES

1. Heat 6-inch crêpe pan over medium-high heat until hot. Brush with ¼ teaspoon safflower oil. Pour 4 tablespoons of batter into center of pan. Gently tilt pan so batter coats entire surface. Cook crêpe 60 seconds or until it begins to bubble.

2. Turn crêpe with metal spatula (when bottom is browned). Lightly brown other side (about 30 seconds).

3. Transfer crêpe to a plate and fill.

RATATOUILLE CRÊPES

These whole wheat crêpes are thin, briefly cooked pancakes rolled around a slightly spicy filling of tomatoes, eggplant, and bell peppers. Ratatouille Crêpes combine two French recipes into one delightful and tasty dish.

- 2 *cups chopped eggplant (peeled or unpeeled)*
- 1 *onion, sliced thinly*
- 1 *clove garlic, minced*
- 2 *red bell peppers, seeded and chopped coarsely*
- 2 *medium zucchini, sliced into rounds*
- 3 *large tomatoes, cored and chopped coarsely*
- 1 *tablespoon chopped fresh basil*
- 2 *tablespoons safflower oil, or as needed*
- ½ *cup grated low-calorie Monterey jack cheese*

Crêpe Batter

- ¾ *cup whole wheat or white pastry flour*
- 1¼ *cups nonfat milk*
- 2 *eggs, beaten*

1. Prepare Crêpe Batter. Combine eggplant, onion, garlic, bell peppers, zucchini, tomatoes, and basil in a stockpot or Dutch oven and cook over medium heat until soft (about 25 minutes).

2. While ratatouille is cooking, heat 1 teaspoon of the safflower oil in a crêpe pan or small skillet and ladle into it 2 to 3 tablespoons of batter. Tilt pan to allow batter to evenly coat surface of pan. Cook crêpe over medium-high heat and flip it when it begins to bubble and brown. Cook 30 seconds on other side, then flip onto a plate. Use more safflower oil, as needed (up to two tablespoons), to grease the crêpe pan.

3. To assemble crêpes, spoon ½ cup of ratatouille vegetable mixture into the center of each crêpe; roll and place seam side down in a baking dish. Sprinkle crêpes with cheese and broil until cheese melts. Serve hot.

Serves 6.

Crêpe Batter In a blender combine flour, milk, and eggs at high speed for 30 seconds.

Makes 12 to 15 crêpes.

<u>Note</u> Crêpes can be made ahead and frozen, and the filling will keep for about one week in the refrigerator.

Preparation time: 25 minutes
Calories per serving: 223
Cooking time: 30 minutes

BROCCOLI-RICOTTA SOUFFLÉ

Adapted from a recipe by James Beard, this easy dish demystifies soufflé making. *Soufflé* derives from the French word for *to breathe* or *to whisper,* and a soufflé is literally holding its breath with trapped air produced during the cooking process. These are sturdy soufflés, especially if cooked in ramekins, or individual soufflé dishes. Try to cook the dish just before serving so it stays light.

- 1 teaspoon safflower oil, plus safflower oil for greasing baking dish
- ½ cup minced onion
- 1 cup cooked broccoli stems and florets, chopped finely
- 2 cups part-skim ricotta cheese
- ⅓ cup grated part-skim mozzarella cheese
- ½ cup grated Parmesan cheese
- 4 eggs, separated

1. Preheat oven to 375° F. Lightly grease 6 ramekins or one 1½-quart soufflé dish with small amount of safflower oil.

2. Heat oil in a skillet and sauté onion until soft but not browned. Remove from heat and stir in broccoli, cheeses, and egg yolks.

3. Beat egg whites until soft peaks form; fold into broccoli mixture. Spoon carefully into prepared soufflé dish or ramekins.

4. Place on baking sheet (to make carrying easier) and bake until lightly browned and puffy (25 to 40 minutes). Serve immediately.

Serves 6.

Calories per serving: 234
Preparation time: 20 minutes
Baking time: 25–40 minutes

Bring Paris to the kitchen with this trio of French dishes: a tangy, herb-scented French bean salad (see page 46), served chilled; a spinach soufflé (see page 60) rolled around a cheese filling; and savory Ratatouille Crêpes.

These refined Vegetarian Sushi Rolls are stuffed with bright strips of vegetables and served with a tongue-tingling Wasabi-Ginger Dipping Sauce. They are delicious with Szechwan Noodles (see page 47) and Kombu Miso Soup (see page 31).

VEGETARIAN SUSHI ROLLS

The word *sushi* means specially seasoned rice, which is often wrapped in toasted *nori* (seaweed). You can fill sushi rolls with a variety of foods, from traditional Japanese ingredients to California-style crab and avocado. When cooking the rice, add extra water to make it sticky. Serve sushi at room temperature—soon after rolling, before the rice begins to soften the nori.

   3 cups cooked brown or
       white rice
  ¼ cup rice vinegar
 1½ tablespoons dry sherry
   3 tablespoons honey
   2 teaspoons salt or herbal salt
       substitute
   6 sheets of toasted nori
   1 firm cucumber, peeled, seeded
       and cut into long strips
   2 carrots, peeled and cut into
       thin strips
   2 red bell peppers, seeded and
       cut into thin strips

Wasabi-Ginger Dipping Sauce

  ¼ cup prepared wasabi (mix
       2 tablespoons powdered
       wasabi with 2 tablespoons
       cold water to form a paste)
   3 tablespoons low-sodium
       tamari or soy sauce
   3 tablespoons grated daikon

1. In a large bowl place cooked rice. In a saucepan over high heat, cook vinegar, sherry, honey, and salt for 5 minutes, stirring occasionally. Pour over rice to make sticky and stir.

2. Lay out the six sheets of nori and spread an equal amount of sushi rice mixture over each, extending rice almost to edges. Lay a strip of each vegetable along the length of the rice.

3. Roll sushi tightly to form a cylinder, then slice into six rounds.

Serves 6.

Wasabi-Ginger Dipping Sauce

Mix ingredients together and serve as dipping sauce with sushi.

Calories per serving: 184
Preparation time: 45 minutes

BURGERS AND CROQUETTES

Following are some delightful recipes for low-calorie vegetable burgers and croquettes that fit easily into lunch and light supper menus.

TOFU SLOPPY JOES ON WHEAT ROLLS WITH OVEN-BAKED FRENCH FRIES

An excellent low-calorie substitute for ground beef, this crumbled tofu mixture is reminiscent of the sloppy joes that we all loved as children. Serve with Oven-Baked French Fries and coleslaw.

- 1 teaspoon safflower oil
- 2 tablespoons dry sherry
- 1 onion, finely chopped
- ½ cup minced green bell pepper
- 2 cloves garlic, minced
- ⅓ cup whole wheat bread crumbs
- 2 cups firm tofu, drained and crumbled
- 1 teaspoon low-sodium tamari or soy sauce
- 1 teaspoon nutritional yeast (yellow flakes)
  Herbal salt substitute and freshly ground black pepper, to taste
- 2 cups tomato sauce
- 1 teaspoon cayenne pepper, or to taste
- ½ teaspoon ground cumin
- 6 whole wheat hamburger buns

Oven-Baked French Fries

- 4 russet potatoes or 8 red potatoes (unpeeled)
- ½ teaspoon safflower oil, for greasing baking sheet

1. In a skillet heat oil and sherry; sauté onion over medium heat until soft but not browned.

2. Add bell pepper and garlic and cook until pepper is soft.

3. Add bread crumbs, tofu, tamari, yeast, and salt substitute and pepper; mix well, cooking 3 minutes more to blend flavors.

4. Remove from heat and add tomato sauce, cayenne, and cumin. Lightly toast insides of hamburger buns, and fill with sloppy joe mixture.

Serves 6.

Oven-Baked French Fries

1. Preheat oven to 250° F. Slice potatoes into French fry strips and place on lightly greased baking sheet.

2. Bake for 20 minutes and turn over when bottoms of fries begin to brown. Cook until lightly browned on all sides, and serve with Tofu Sloppy Joes on Wheat Rolls.

> *Calories per serving: 392*
> *Preparation time: 45 minutes*
> *Cooking time: 45 minutes*

PECAN BURGERS

About 12 years ago an enterprising young cook made fantastic vegetarian burgers and sold them on the streets of a small mill town on the East Coast. The original recipe follows and is sure to appeal to any hamburger lover. If you like, serve on whole wheat buns garnished with tomato slices, red onion rings, and lettuce.

- 1 cup ground pecans (pecan meal)
- ½ cup wheat germ
- ½ cup wheat bran or oat bran
- ½ onion, grated
- ½ large carrot, grated
- 1 tablespoon dark sesame oil
- 1 teaspoon low-sodium tamari or soy sauce
  Oil, for greasing skillet

1. In a large bowl mix all ingredients and form patties.

2. In a lightly greased skillet, fry lightly on both sides until browned.

Makes 4 burgers, 4 servings.

> *Calories per serving: 332*
> * (not including buns)*
> *Preparation time: 15 minutes*
> *Cooking time: 25 minutes*

BEAN BURGERS

These hearty burgers are great after a football game or for a tailgate party. Serve them on whole wheat hamburger buns or English muffins, accompanied by a platter of lettuce leaves, red onion slices, and stone-ground mustard.

- ¼ cup finely minced onion
- ⅓ cup diced celery
- 1 tablespoon minced garlic
- 1 teaspoon safflower oil, plus oil for greasing
- 2 cups cooked and mashed chick-peas
- ½ cup Mary's Chunky Tomato Sauce With Fresh Basil (see page 109)
- ¼ cup cooked and mashed red or russet potato
- 1½ cups whole wheat bread crumbs or crushed whole wheat cracker crumbs
- ¼ teaspoon thyme
- 1 teaspoon minced fresh basil
  Pinch ground rosemary
  Freshly ground pepper, to taste
  Herbal salt substitute, to taste

1. In a medium-sized heavy skillet, sauté onion, celery, and garlic in safflower oil until soft but not browned (5 to 8 minutes). Add chick-peas and tomato sauce and cook 3 minutes over medium heat, stirring often. Remove from heat.

2. Preheat oven to 400° F. Lightly oil a 9- by 12-inch baking sheet.

3. In a large bowl mix together the sautéed vegetables, potato, bread crumbs, thyme, basil, rosemary, pepper, and salt substitute. Form into 4 patties.

4. Place on baking sheet and bake until browned and firm (about 15 minutes per side). Serve hot.

Makes 4 burgers, 4 servings.

> *Calories per serving: 241*
> * (not including buns)*
> *Preparation time: 20 minutes*
> *Cooking time: 34–40 minutes*

This light Ricotta-Spinach-Mushroom Quiche is made from mushrooms, spinach, green onions, low-fat cheese and savory herbs baked in a whole wheat pie crust. Serve with a crisp green salad.

TASTY TARTS AND PIES

Most cuisines have their own versions of savory tarts and pies: pasty in England, calzone and pizza in Italy, quiche in France. Unfortunately, most traditional crusts are laden with high-calorie ingredients. Here are a few recipes that have been adapted to low-calorie cuisine and still pass the good taste test.

MEXICAN CORN PIE

This low-calorie version of tamale pie is a hearty casserole layered with a cornmeal crust and chili-flavored beans and vegetables. Cook it ahead if you like—it freezes beautifully.

- 2 teaspoons safflower oil
- 1 medium onion, chopped
- 3 cloves garlic, minced
- 1 cup seeded and chopped red bell pepper
- ½ cup diced carrot
- 3 cups cooked kidney beans (approximately 2 cups raw)
- 1 cup thick tomato sauce
- 2 teaspoons chili powder
- 1 teaspoon cumin
- 2 tablespoons white wine

Pie Crust

- 2 cups finely ground yellow cornmeal
- ½ cup whole wheat or white pastry flour
- 2 teaspoons baking powder
- 1 teaspoon herbal salt substitute
- ½ cup water, or as needed
  Oil, for greasing baking dish

1. Prepare Pie Crust. Heat oil in skillet; add onion and sauté over medium heat until soft, but not browned. Add garlic, bell pepper, and carrot and cook 5 minutes, stirring frequently.

2. Add remaining ingredients and cover. Simmer until vegetables are tender. Spoon filling into prepared baking dish and gently lay the top crust onto it. Press edges of two crusts together to seal.

3. Bake until brown and bubbly (about 40 minutes). Serve hot.

Serves 8 to 10.

Pie Crust

1. Preheat oven to 350° F. Mix all ingredients except oil for greasing and knead until smooth. Lightly grease a 9- by 12-inch baking dish; pat half the dough into the bottom of the dish.

2. Spread a long sheet of waxed paper on countertop and pat remaining dough onto it, roughly in the shape of a 9- by 12-inch rectangle. Set aside until you have prepared filling.

Calories per serving: 221
Preparation time: 30 minutes
Cooking time: 55 minutes

FRENCH ONION TART WITH MUSHROOMS AND HERBS

Every low-calorie diet can include an occasional treat. This recipe calls for a rich French cheese, but you can make a softer quiche with less calories by substituting farmer cheese for the Gruyère. Onion tarts are very common in French bakeries, and the secret of the caramelized onions is in the slow cooking. Once baked, this tart can be frozen.

- *2 teaspoons safflower oil*
- *¼ cup dry sherry*
- *2 cups thinly sliced onions, preferably sweet onions*
- *½ cup sliced mushrooms*
- *1 teaspoon minced fresh tarragon (optional)*
- *½ cup nonfat milk*
- *¼ teaspoon grated nutmeg*
- *½ teaspoon white pepper*
- *2 eggs*
- *1 whole wheat pie shell (storebought), unbaked*
- *½ cup grated Gruyère cheese*

1. Preheat oven to 400° F. Heat oil and sherry in a skillet and add onions. Sauté for 20 minutes, at medium heat, stirring frequently. Onions will become very soft, almost mushy, then begin to lightly brown.

2. Add mushrooms and tarragon (if used) and cook 3 minutes. Remove from heat.

3. In a small bowl, beat milk, nutmeg, pepper, and eggs.

4. Spoon onion mixture into pie shell, sprinkle with cheese, and carefully pour milk-egg mixture on top of them.

5. Bake tart until it sets and becomes lightly browned (about 40 minutes). Let it cool slightly and slice into 8 wedges. Serve hot or cold.

Serves 8.

Calories per serving: 218
Preparation time: 20 minutes
Cooking time: 25 minutes
Baking time: 40 minutes

RICOTTA-SPINACH-MUSHROOM QUICHE

Spinach is a winter vegetable, at its best between January and May. Look for large, fresh, green leaves. Spinach is an excellent source for vitamins A and C and iron and calcium, making this dish nutritious as well as flavorful. This quiche is best eaten after it has a chance to cool and solidify, since it is very soft when just out of the oven. Enjoy it cold, the next day, with a green salad and a light soup.

- *2 cups chopped spinach leaves (well-washed and dried between paper towels)*
- *1 cup sliced mushrooms*
- *¼ cup chopped green onions*
- *1 whole wheat pie shell (storebought), unbaked*
- *1 cup nonfat milk*
- *2 cups part-skim ricotta cheese*
- *3 eggs, beaten*
- *¼ teaspoon grated nutmeg*
- *¼ teaspoon dried tarragon*
- *⅛ teaspoon rosemary*
- *Freshly ground pepper, to taste*

1. Preheat oven to 400° F. In a bowl mix spinach, mushrooms, and green onions. Spoon mixture into pie shell.

2. Mix milk, ricotta, and eggs; then stir in nutmeg, tarragon, rosemary, and pepper. Pour over spinach mixture.

3. Bake quiche until it sets and lightly browns (30 to 40 minutes). Let cool before slicing. Quiche may be served hot or cold.

Serves 8.

Calories per serving: 235
Preparation time: 25 minutes
Baking time: 40 minutes

FRENCH CANDLELIGHT DINNER FOR FOUR

French Onion and Garlic Soup

French Buckwheat Croquettes With Miso Sauce

Steamed Carrots and Asparagus Tips

Limestone and Bibb Lettuce Salad

Strawberries in Orange Shells

Nonalcoholic Sparkling Blush Wine

The French have always been romantics, and this menu sets the mood for a warm, relaxing evening. Use fine linen, china, fresh flowers, and candles on the table. Make as much of this dinner as possible ahead of time, and then enjoy a glass of wine with your dinner companions. Steam the fresh vegetables and toss the salad right before serving. You'll be happy to learn that the entire menu contains less than 700 calories per serving. The menu serves four.

FRENCH ONION AND GARLIC SOUP

The secret of really good onion soup is to sauté the sliced onions very slowly so that their natural sweetness emerges. Onions cooked too quickly or at high heat have a stronger, more bitter taste. This popular onion soup recipe uses this technique.

- 1 teaspoon safflower oil
- 3 large yellow onions, sliced into very thin rounds
- 3 cups defatted Chicken or Beef Stock (see page 31)
- 4 cloves garlic, minced
- 1 bay leaf, crushed
- ¼ cup minced parsley
- 1 teaspoon dried basil
  Herbal salt substitute, if needed
- 4 zwieback crackers or sliced French bread, toasted
- ¼ cup grated Parmesan cheese

1. In a large stockpot over medium heat, heat oil and sauté onions, stirring constantly. Add 1 cup of the stock and cover; simmer until onions are extremely soft and begin to brown (about 20 minutes).

2. Add garlic and herbs and remaining stock. Cover, bring to a boil, then lower heat and cook 25 minutes.

3. Taste for seasoning; add salt substitute, if needed. To serve, ladle into four ovenproof bowls. Float one zwieback cracker on each bowl of soup. Sprinkle each serving with 1 tablespoon Parmesan cheese. Broil until cheese browns.

Serves 4.

> *Calories per serving: 159*
> *Preparation time: 20 minutes*
> *Cooking time: 55 minutes*

FRENCH BUCKWHEAT CROQUETTES WITH MISO SAUCE

This recipe comes from French macrobiotic cooking, which has strong Japanese influences. These patties can be made up to two days ahead. Since this recipe makes enough for six, refrigerate the extra patties for lunch the next day.

- ½ cup buckwheat groats
- 2 cups boiling water
- 1 teaspoon herbal salt substitute
- ½ cup whole wheat flour, or more, if needed
- 1 teaspoon safflower oil, plus safflower oil for frying
- 1 small onion, minced
- 3 green onions (including greens), chopped well
- ½ cup chopped parsley
- 1 beaten egg

Miso Sauce

- 2 cloves garlic, minced
- 1 teaspoon dark sesame oil
- 2 teaspoons whole wheat or all-purpose flour
- 1 cup nonfat milk
- 3 teaspoons light-colored miso (fermented soybean paste)
- 2 tablespoons hot water
- ½ teaspoon Dijon mustard
- ¼ cup grated low-calorie Monterey jack cheese

1. In a deep saucepan lightly toast groats by heating over medium heat until they lightly brown and emit a nutlike aroma.

2. Add the boiling water to groats. Add salt substitute and cook mixture over medium heat until groats become very soft (15 to 20 minutes). Let cool and stir in ½ cup flour.

3. Meanwhile, heat oil in a skillet and sauté onion for several minutes. Add green onions and parsley and remove from heat.

4. Mix onion mixture with buckwheat and stir in egg.

5. Using flour to thicken the mixture, if needed, form into small patties. Fry lightly on both sides in safflower oil (about 1 tablespoon).

Serves 4.

Miso Sauce

1. Place garlic and oil in a medium skillet; sauté 1 minute over medium heat. Add flour; cook, stirring, for 2 more minutes.

2. Slowly pour in milk, stirring with whisk until sauce thickens. In a separate bowl mix miso with the hot water, stirring until very smooth.

3. Add miso, mustard, and cheese to sauce. Serve hot over croquettes.

> *Calories per serving: 210*
> *Preparation time: 20 minutes*
> *Cooking time: 45 minutes*

STRAWBERRIES IN ORANGE SHELLS

In this delicate dessert, halved oranges are scooped out and then filled with a whipped strawberry mixture. For best flavor, make the dish no more than a few hours before serving.

- 2 large navel oranges
- 3 cups sliced strawberries
- ½ cup Neufchâtel cheese
- 1 cup nonfat, plain yogurt
- 3 tablespoons maple syrup
- 1 teaspoon nutmeg
- ¼ teaspoon ground cardamom
  Mint leaves and freshly grated nutmeg, for garnish

1. Halve oranges and, with a metal spoon, scoop out orange pulp (reserve for another use).

2. In a blender, briefly purée remaining ingredients, except garnishes. The idea is to mash the strawberries without destroying their texture and to keep from overblending the cheese.

3. Spoon puréed mixture into orange shells, mounding slightly over rims. Place on a plate and chill for 1 hour. Garnish with mint leaves and freshly grated nutmeg.

Serves 4.

> *Calories per serving: 251*
> *Preparation time: 20 minutes*
> *Chilling time: 1 hour*

Flavors from France and Japan combine in these buckwheat croquettes with miso sauce, served with green salad, French onion soup, and strawberry mousse.

Chicken can be prepared in many low-calorie ways, such as marinated and grilled, stewed with vegetables, or baked in parchment with wine and herbs.

Chicken & Lean Meats

Chicken, lean beef, lamb, and veal should be included in your low-calorie menus for their nutritional value. But these meats need special attention in order to qualify as low-calorie. Many of the recipes in this chapter focus on low-calorie cooking techniques—broiling, grilling, stir-frying—and new ideas for creating low-calorie sauces using sherries and other wines (see page 83). The chapter also includes a guide to basic stir-frying techniques (see page 79) and step-by-step photographs showing how to cut up a whole chicken (see page 76). A Dinner From the Far East (see page 85), featuring Hunan-Style Chicken Stir-fry With Vegetables, ends the chapter.

The aromas of thyme, sage, and tarragon combine with pungent lemon to create this baked lemon chicken. Serve with roasted green peppers and rice pilaf to create a hearty meal that is great for an afternoon picnic or a summer supper.

INTERNATIONAL CHICKEN ENTRÉES

Try baking chicken breasts or sliced lean beef *en papillote* or in parchment, which is a lightweight cooking paper that comes in a roll like aluminum foil. Add some fresh herbs, a little wine, and lemon slices, and 20 minutes later you'll have a hot, delicious main course.

Another idea: Try marinating, which can be a dieter's boon since it gives flavors and richness without adding calories. Begin with an overnight basting in some wine, spice, or herb mixture, and the next day just pop the meat into the oven. The marinade can be reduced by cooking rapidly at high heat, and served as a low-calorie sauce.

Select chicken carefully for lowest calories. The lighter-colored meat is usually the least fattening. You can also reduce calories by skinning chicken before cooking and skimming any accumulated fat off cooking liquor with a gravy separator or with a piece of bread floating on top.

Most of the following dishes can be made ahead, wrapped well, and frozen. Let frozen chicken come to room temperature before cooking, either by placing it in a microwave for a few minutes or by letting the meat thaw in the refrigerator overnight.

Without the extra fat of the skin, chicken is easy to overcook. The meat is usually done when a sharp knife, inserted into a dark meat section, such as the thigh, produces juices that run clear instead of pink. Moist, tender chicken will have a slightly crisp exterior and will burst with juice when pierced.

CHICKEN NIÇOISE

Niçoise dishes are those cooked in the style of Nice, a small town in southern France where fragrant herbs grow wild on the hillsides above the sea. This marinated chicken dish captures the flavor of that sun-drenched area and has been adapted for low-calorie cooking. Serve Chicken Niçoise with crusty French bread, a crisp green salad, and a dessert of fresh fruit.

- 2 teaspoons olive oil
- 4 half-breasts of chicken, skinned
- 2 teaspoons saffron threads, soaked in 2 tablespoons dry sherry
- 3 cloves garlic, peeled and halved
- ½ teaspoon dried tarragon
- ¼ teaspoon dried thyme
    Pinch dried sage
- 2 crushed bay leaves
- 5 plum tomatoes, coarsely chopped
- 5 Greek olives, pitted and chopped
- 1¼ cups white wine
- 1½ cups defatted Chicken Stock (see page 31)
- 1 teaspoon herbal salt substitute

1. In a Dutch oven or heavy skillet, heat oil and lightly brown chicken pieces over medium-high heat.

2. Add remaining ingredients to skillet and bring to a boil. Lower heat, cover, and simmer until chicken is cooked (about 40 minutes).

3. Remove chicken to a serving platter and keep warm in the oven. Reduce cooking liquor by boiling rapidly over high heat for 5 minutes. Pour over chicken and serve.

Serves 4.

Calories per serving: 219
Preparation time: 20 minutes
Marinating time: 30 minutes
Cooking time: 55 minutes

LEMON CHICKEN

This version of a Greek dish uses both fresh and dried herbs, the juice from several fresh lemons, and a whole roasting chicken. For a Thanksgiving-style entrée you can stuff the cavity of the chicken with more of the herbs or a light wheat bread stuffing. Serve with light soup, salad, and a fruit dessert.

- 1 whole roasting chicken, skinned
- 1 tablespoon dried thyme
- 1 teaspoon dried sage, crushed
- ½ teaspoon freshly ground pepper
- 3 lemons
- 2 tablespoons minced fresh tarragon, if available, or 1 tablespoon dried tarragon

1. Preheat oven to 375° F. Wash roasting chicken and pat dry. Place breast side up in a large roasting pan or deep baking dish.

2. Rub thyme, sage, and pepper over entire surface of chicken. Slice lemons in half and squeeze the juice through a sieve onto chicken (the sieve traps the seeds). Sprinkle tarragon over chicken.

3. Lightly tuck a large piece of aluminum foil over and around the top of the chicken. Bake until juices run clear when leg is pierced with a sharp knife (about 35 minutes). Remove aluminum foil for last 5 minutes of baking. Serve hot.

Serves 8.

Calories per serving: 160
Preparation time: 20 minutes
Cooking time: 40 minutes

BRUNSWICK STEW

Brought to you from a quaint New England tavern, where it is served as a Sunday staple, Brunswick Stew starts with vegetables and a tender roasting chicken and cooks over low heat. Make this recipe ahead and freeze in 1-quart containers for an easy and delicious Sunday dinner for family and friends. Serve with a green salad, crusty rolls, and a light fruit dessert.

- 2 teaspoons safflower oil
- 2 large onions, coarsely chopped
- 1 cup dry sherry
- 4 cups stewed tomatoes
- 2 cups frozen or fresh lima beans
- 3 large red potatoes, cubed
- 4 cups frozen or fresh corn kernels
- 1 roasting chicken (6 lb), cut up and skinned
- 2 tablespoons herbal salt substitute
    Freshly ground pepper, to taste
    Chopped parsley, for garnish (optional)

1. In a large stockpot or Dutch oven, heat oil and slowly sauté onions until soft and lightly browned.

2. Add sherry, tomatoes, lima beans, potatoes, and corn and cook 5 minutes.

3. Add chicken, salt substitute, pepper, and enough water to cover chicken. Bring to a boil.

4. Lower heat and let stew simmer, uncovered, for 45 minutes. Add more water when needed.

5. To serve, ladle chicken pieces into shallow soup bowls, top with vegetables and stock, and garnish with chopped parsley, if desired.

Serves 8.

Calories per serving: 387
Preparation time: 15 minutes
Cooking time: 45 minutes

CHICKEN MOLE IN BURRITOS

Mole (pronounced MOH-lay) is
a thick, chocolate sauce often served
over chicken or turkey. Once a delicacy enjoyed only by Aztec leaders,
this chocolate dish has long been
a part of Mexican haute cuisine.
Adapted for low-calorie eating, this
mole recipe uses carob, cinnamon,
and ginger for delicate seasoning
instead of chocolate. You can make
the chicken mole filling ahead of
time, and even freeze it, but assemble
the burritos right before serving for
best flavor.

    2 teaspoons safflower oil
    1 cup chopped onion
    2 cloves garlic, minced
    1 tablespoon roasted carob
       powder
    1 teaspoon dried oregano
    ½ teaspoon cinnamon
    1 teaspoon grated fresh ginger
    1 teaspoon chili powder
    ½ teaspoon ground cloves
    ¼ teaspoon nutmeg
    ½ teaspoon allspice
    1 teaspoon cumin
    4 cups shredded white chicken,
       skinned
    1 cup defatted Chicken Stock
       (see page 31)
    ¼ cup tomato paste
    2 tablespoons almonds, ground
       finely
       Hot sauce, to taste
    6 flour tortillas, preferably
       whole wheat
       Plain, nonfat yogurt, for
       garnish

1. In a skillet heat oil and sauté
onion over medium heat until onion
is soft. Add garlic, carob, oregano,
cinnamon, ginger, chili powder,
cloves, nutmeg, allspice, and cumin
and cook over medium heat for
5 minutes, stirring frequently.

2. Add chicken, stock, tomato paste,
and almonds, and bring to a boil.
Simmer over medium heat, uncovered, for 10 minutes (mixture should
thicken). Add hot sauce.

3. In a slow oven warm tortillas. Fill
each tortilla with ¾ cup of chicken
mixture, and roll. Serve with nonfat,
plain yogurt as garnish.

Serves 6.

Calories per serving: 307
Preparation time: 40 minutes
Cooking time: 15 minutes

POULET EN SAC

One of the easiest ways to cook a
chicken or turkey is simply to place it
in a lightly buttered brown bag. (Be
sure not to use a bag with ink
printing, which may be toxic.) The
slightly porous paper allows air to
escape, but moisture is retained and
the bird comes out juicy and tender,
and baked to a golden brown. *En sac*
is the "country" ancestor of the
fancier *en papillote* (parchment)
cooking method.

    1 large roasting chicken,
       skinned
    1 large onion, quartered
    1 stalk celery, quartered
    ¼ cup chopped celery leaves
    1 yam or sweet potato, scrubbed
       and quartered
    1 cup seasoned bread crumbs or
       dry stuffing (optional)
    1 apple (optional)
    ¼ cup white wine
    2 teaspoons dried thyme
    2 crushed bay leaves
    2 teaspoons herbal salt
       substitute
    1 teaspoon frehly ground pepper
    2 tablespoons butter, softened

1. Preheat oven to 325° F. Place
chicken in a deep roasting pan and
stuff cavity of chicken with onion,
celery, celery leaves, and yam. Add
bread crumbs, if used. Place whole
apple, if used, in mouth of cavity
to seal.

2. Mix wine, thyme, bay leaves, salt
substitute, and pepper. Rub on surface
of chicken.

3. Butter the inside of a large brown
bag (choose a bag without printing).
Carefully place the stuffed chicken
inside the bag (it should fit loosely)
and seal end of bag by rolling tightly.
Place bagged, stuffed chicken in
roasting pan.

4. Roast chicken until a knife point
inserted in the thigh of chicken produces juices that are clear rather than
pink (45 minutes to 1 hour). Tear off
bag, remove stuffing, place chicken
on a platter, and serve, surrounded by
cooked vegetables and stuffing.

Serves 8.

Calories per serving: 169
Preparation time: 15 minutes
Cooking time: 45 minutes–1 hour

SPICY SALSA CHICKEN

This recipe is great for a picnic
lunch, served with Green Gazpacho
(see page 39), a crisp salad, and
Wine-Basted Pears (see page 115) for
dessert. Choose a bottled salsa that
suits your taste buds for hotness: It
will not lose its spicy flavor during
the cooking process.

    4 half-breasts of chicken,
       skinned
    1 cup salsa
    1 tablespoon rice vinegar
    1 tablespoon minced cilantro
       Lemon slices or yellow chiles,
       for garnish

1. Preheat oven to 375° F. Place
chicken breasts in a medium-sized
baking dish.

2. Mix salsa, vinegar, and cilantro.
Spoon over chicken.

3. Bake chicken for 20 to 25 minutes, uncovered. Serve hot or cold,
garnished with lemon slices.

Serves 4.

Calories per serving: 117
Preparation time: 10 minutes
Cooking time: 20–25 minutes

GRILLED CHICKEN IN SWEET MARINADE

A pleasing Asian dish, in which strips of chicken are marinated in a soy-ginger sauce and then grilled lightly with vegetables, this should be made right before serving. However, the chicken and vegetables can be cut ahead and stored in plastic bags until cooking time.

    2 *boned, skinned whole breasts of chicken*
    ⅓ *cup low-sodium tamari or soy sauce*
    2 *teaspoons dark sesame oil*
    2 *teaspoons grated fresh ginger*
    2 *teaspoons honey*
       Juice of 2 limes
    ¼ *teaspoon cayenne pepper*
    2 *red bell peppers, seeded and cut into quarters*
    2 *green bell peppers, seeded and cut into quarters*
    1 *cup pineapple chunks, preferably fresh*
    4 *cups cooked brown rice (optional)*

1. Cut chicken into long, thin strips. Place the strips in a shallow, non-reactive pan.

2. Mix tamari, sesame oil, ginger, honey, lime juice, and cayenne and pour over chicken, tossing well. Let marinate for 2 hours.

3. Preheat broiler. During the last 15 minutes of marinating time, toss in bell peppers and pineapple chunks, coating well with marinade.

4. While chicken and vegetables are marinating, soak 12 bamboo skewers in a shallow pan of salted water for 15 minutes (2 tablespoons salt to 2 cups water). This will prevent skewers from burning during grilling.

5. Skewer chicken strips, alternating with pineapple and bell peppers. Grill on both sides until browned, basting occasionally with the marinade. Serve over rice, if desired.

Serves 4.

> *Calories per serving: 181*
> *Preparation time: 30 minutes*
> *Marinating time: 2 hours*
> *Cooking time: 15 minutes*

Create a fiesta of flavors and colors with this salsa-baked chicken, spiced with chopped cilantro.

CUTTING UP A WHOLE CHICKEN

All raw chicken, whether whole or cut up, should be washed and cleaned. Remove any unappetizing fat, cartilage, or other matter.

Remove innards (neck and giblets) from cavity. Tear away any loose or large pieces of fat around both openings and from skin around neck. Insert hand into cavity and remove any tendons and fat that will pull away. Wash bird under cold running water, inside cavity and out. Pat dry with paper towels.

Cutting up a whole fresh chicken is in some ways similar to carving a cooked one, except that you are cutting through bone, which is not as easy to sever as a joint. You will need a boning knife, a heavy 8- or 10-inch chef's knife, and poultry shears. When done, you will have eight serving pieces: two breast halves; two thighs; two drumsticks; and two wings.

2. *After the joint has been exposed, separate leg from body by cutting through the skin to joint and severing leg at joint. Repeat for other leg.*

5. *To halve breast, cut through the breastbone with a chef's knife.*

3. *Separate thigh and drumstick by cutting into leg at joint with boning knife; sever completely.*

6. *Sever wing from back by cutting through at joint with chef's knife. Reserve back for stock.*

1. *To expose the joint, hold on to the body with one hand and pull the leg away from the body with the other.*

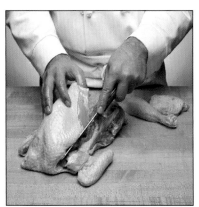

4. *To remove whole breast from rib cage and wings, insert knife or poultry shears at the dividing line between breast and rib cage, beginning at wing joint. Cut along the edge of the rib cage, cutting through the cartilage between wing and breast. Repeat on other side; breast is now completely severed.*

7. *When completed, cup-up chicken consists of two wings, two breast halves, two thighs, two drumsticks, plus the back.*

SIMPLE BAKED CHICKEN WITH ORANGE AND CUMIN

This Middle Eastern recipe calls for vegetables, fresh orange juice and rind, and a currylike medley of spices. Bake it ahead of time and warm it up before serving. This dish keeps well frozen or can be refrigerated for up to four days, if covered tightly with plastic wrap.

1 large roasting chicken, skinned
1 cup fresh orange juice
½ cup dry sherry
½ cup defatted Chicken Stock (see page 31)
1 cup sliced onion
¼ cup minced green onion
½ cup julienned carrot
⅓ cup currants
2 tablespoons grated orange rind
1 teaspoon ground cumin
1 teaspoon paprika
¼ teaspoon cayenne pepper
4 cups cooked rice (optional)

1. Preheat oven to 350° F. Place chicken in a shallow roasting pan and prick with a skewer to allow juices to penetrate when marinating.

2. Mix remaining ingredients except rice and pour over chicken. Marinate for 2 hours or overnight, turning and basting occasionally.

3. Roast, in marinade, for 45 minutes. Remove chicken and vegetables to a serving platter and keep warm in low oven.

4. Reduce marinade by boiling rapidly over high heat until one half of original volume. Pour sauce over chicken.

5. Serve hot, with rice, if desired.

Serves 4.

Calories per serving: 247
Preparation time: 20 minutes
Marinating time: 2 hours
Baking time: 45 minutes

CASHEW CHICKEN

A popular dish served in many Chinese restaurants, this low-calorie version can be accompanied by cooked brown rice and eaten with chopsticks. Cashew Chicken can be made the day before and reheated, but it doesn't freeze very well.

1 teaspoon dark sesame oil
1 tablespoon safflower oil
¼ cup dry sherry
1 cup sliced green onions (including greens)
1 red bell pepper, seeded and julienned
1 cup cauliflower florets
2 carrots, julienned
3 cups cooked chicken breast, sliced into thin strips
1 tablespoon arrowroot powder mixed with 3 tablespoons cold water
2 tablespoons low-sodium tamari or soy sauce
2 tablespoons oyster sauce
1 teaspoon honey
½ cup unsalted whole cashews
1 cup trimmed snow peas, left whole
4 cups cooked brown rice (optional)

1. In a wok or skillet over medium-high heat, combine oils and sherry and stir-fry green onions for 2 minutes. Add bell pepper, cauliflower, and carrots, and continue cooking for 5 minutes, stirring frequently.

2. Add chicken and cook, covered, for 2 minutes.

3. Add arrowroot slurry, tamari, oyster sauce, and honey. Cook until arrowroot begins to thicken sauce (about 2 minutes), stirring frequently.

4. Add cashews and snow peas, cover, and let steam until snow peas become bright green (about 1 minute). Serve hot, over rice, if desired.

Serves 6.

Calories per serving: 252
Preparation time: 25 minutes
Cooking time: 10 minutes

MALAYSIAN CURRIED CHICKEN SALAD

This refreshing summer salad is easy to prepare, can be made up to 24 hours ahead of time, and is best served at room temperature or slightly chilled. Served after Chilled Curried Zucchini Soup (see page 37), it forms an easy to prepare, low-calorie entrée for an alfresco summer lunch.

2 cooked whole chicken breasts, skinned and diced
¼ cup raisins
¼ cup sliced almonds
½ cup crushed, drained pineapple
⅓ cup low-calorie mayonnaise
2 tablespoons low-sodium tamari or soy sauce
1 tablespoon curry powder
1 tablespoon lemon juice
4 large lettuce leaves, for lining plates

Combine all ingredients. Serve over lettuce leaves.

Serves 4.

Calories per serving: 250
Preparation time: 15 minutes

1. In a large skillet heat oil; add carrot and stir-fry for 2 minutes over medium-high heat.

2. Add chicken and cook on both sides until lightly browned (about 10 minutes).

3. Add tamari, honey, green onion, garlic, ginger, and pepper. Simmer, covered, until chicken is tender. Serve hot.

Serves 4.

Calories per serving: 164
Preparation time: 25 minutes
Cooking time: 20–25 minutes

GINGER-TAMARI CHICKEN

Slightly spicy, slightly exotic, this marinated chicken is perfect to serve with fresh fruit salad or steamed red potatoes. To dress it up for company, garnish with slices of red onion and papaya. Let the chicken marinate several hours or overnight, covered, in the refrigerator.

> 4 *half-breasts of chicken, skinned*
> 2 *tablespoons minced red onion*
> ¼ *cup low-sodium tamari or soy sauce*
> 2 *tablespoons grated fresh ginger*
> 2 *teaspoons dark sesame oil*
> ¼ *cup white wine or dry sherry Pinch dried thyme*

1. Preheat oven to 375° F. Place chicken in a deep baking dish.

2. Mix red onion, tamari, ginger, sesame oil, wine, and thyme and pour over chicken. Let marinate, covered, with plastic wrap, for 3 hours in the refrigerator. Turn and baste every hour so the meat marinates evenly.

3. Bake chicken in marinade until juices run clear when knife tip is inserted (35 to 40 minutes). Remove from marinade and serve.

Serves 4.

Calories per serving: 138
Preparation time: 15 minutes
Marinating time: 3 hours
Baking time: 35–40 minutes

A low-fat and flavorful method of baking, parchment seals in moisture yet allows chicken to brown and crisp. This California recipe combines breasts of chicken with Chardonnay wine, shallots, tarragon, and ripe tomatoes.

KOREAN CHICKEN WITH SOY SAUCE AND GARLIC

An easy-to-prepare picnic recipe, Korean Chicken can become an instant family favorite. Make it ahead and warm it up before serving. It can also be frozen and defrosted for later use. Serve with Kombu Miso Soup (see page 31) and a green salad.

> 2 *teaspoons dark sesame oil*
> ½ *cup julienned carrot*
> 1 *large cut-up roasting chicken (2 to 3 lb), skinned*
> 6 *tablespoons tamari or low-sodium soy sauce*
> 2 *teaspoons honey*
> 3 *tablespoons minced green onion*
> 2 *teaspoons minced garlic*
> 1 *teaspoon grated fresh ginger*
> ¼ *teaspoon freshly ground pepper*

CHICKEN BAKED WITH TOMATOES AND HERBS IN PARCHMENT

A version of Poulet en Sac (see page 74), this chicken baked in parchment is tender, moist, and fragrant with the aroma of herbs. Parchment paper is available now in most supermarkets and is a boon to the low-calorie cook because it allows cooking without extra fat. Packets may be assembled the day before, wrapped in plastic, and stored in the refrigerator until baking time. A packet of chicken is given to each diner at the table.

> 6 *boned whole breasts of chicken, skinned*
> 3 *cups coarsely chopped tomatoes*
> ¼ *cup minced shallot*
> 1 *cup dry white wine, such as a California Chardonnay*
> 2 *tablespoons minced fresh tarragon*
> 2 *tablespoons minced parsley*

1. Preheat oven to 375° F. Lay out 6 sheets of parchment paper on table or counter and place one chicken breast in the center of each. Top each breast with ½ cup tomatoes and 2 teaspoons minced shallot. Add 2 to 3 tablespoons of white wine to each packet and evenly distribute tarragon and parsley on top of breasts.

2. Fold the parchment packets like envelopes, to seal around chicken and vegetables, making sure that wine does not run out.

3. Place sealed packets on baking sheets and bake for 20 minutes. Serve hot.

Serves 6.

Calories per serving: 232
Preparation time: 30 minutes
Cooking time: 20 minutes

LEAN BEEF AND VEAL ENTRÉES

When choosing lean meats, look for uniform color without the white marbling that indicates extra fat. Grocers package ground beef with labels such as extralean—a good buy for the dieter.

Properly cooked beef and veal are slightly resilient to the touch. In hamburger grills, cooks typically press lightly in the center of the burger. Well-done beef bounces back while rare holds the indentation. Pounded veal or thin veal scallops cook very quickly: They are usually done when the edges begin to curl.

MINUTE STEAKS DIANE

This recipe is a perfect dish to cook after a long day, when you have only 15 minutes to prepare a satisfying dinner for an entire hungry family. Minute steaks are thinly pounded slices of lean beef; you can buy them in the freezer section of the supermarket, and they can be kept frozen until ready to use.

> 1 *teaspoon safflower oil*
> 2 *tablespoons chopped green onion*
> 4 *minute steaks (8 oz each)*
> 2 *tablespoons chopped chives*
> 2 *tablespoons Worcestershire sauce*
> 1 *teaspoon low-sodium tamari or soy sauce*

1. In skillet heat oil and sauté green onion over medium-high heat for 1 minute.

2. Add steaks to skillet and brown quickly on both sides. Remove steaks to platter.

3. Add chives, Worcestershire, and tamari to skillet and cook 2 minutes over moderate heat, stirring. Return steaks to pan and heat through. Serve hot.

Serves 4.

Calories per serving: 440
Preparation time: 7 minutes
Cooking time: 5–10 minutes

Basics

STIR-FRYING TECHNIQUES

Stir-frying brings out the full flavor of a sauté without the high calories of other frying methods; less oil is needed due to quick cooking. Stir-frying is usually done at high heat in a wok, which is ideal because it conducts heat quickly and evenly along all surfaces, preventing or scorching of the food. Look for carbon steel woks that include directions on seasoning the metal. Well-seasoned woks require only a little oil to stop food from sticking to the surface.

When stir-frying you should continually toss the food, using a wooden spoon or spatula. This moistens the pieces of food with the cooking liquor and bathes the mixture with cooling air, to prevent burning.

Begin by heating a small amount of oil (1 to 2 teaspoons) plus ¼ cup of wine or sherry in the wok or skillet. Use medium-high to high heat when stir-frying. Let the cooking liquor begin to simmer slightly. Then add the strongest-flavored vegetables (such as onions) and quickly toss with the cooking liquor to coat completely. Add other vegetables when the onions soften.

When stir-frying vegetables with meat or fish, cook the meat or fish first; then remove from heat while vegetables, which have a higher water content, finish cooking. Asian cooks who work with large woks quickly stir-fry the shrimp, chicken, or beef, cooking it just enough to sear the outside, and then push the partially cooked meat to the upper sides of the wok, where it stays warm while the vegetables cook in the bowl part of the wok.

Finally, season the stir-fry and thicken with a slurry of arrowroot powder and water. The successful stir-fry has a bright appearance, a crisp texture, and plenty of seasoning.

VEAL WITH LEMON

Piccata traditionally refers to something piquant, or slightly tart, such as lemon juice or capers. This is a low-calorie adaptation of the traditional Italian recipe of veal piccata. The secret of this recipe is pounding the veal into very thin slices that will melt in your mouth like butter.

- 1 pound veal scallops
- 2 teaspoons safflower oil
- ¾ cup flour
- 2 teaspoons herbal salt substitute
- 1 teaspoon white pepper
- ½ cup lemon juice, preferably fresh
- ⅓ cup minced parsley
- 2 tablespoons capers
- 2 tablespoons minced dill
- ½ lemon, sliced thinly, for garnish

1. Score the top of each veal scallop with a sharp knife. Place each veal scallop between two layers of waxed paper and pound with a meat mallet until very thin and tender.

2. In a skillet heat oil. Mix flour, salt substitute, and pepper on a shallow plate. Dredge veal scallops in flour; then lightly fry them. The thin veal scallops will curl and brown when they are done—do not overcook. Place veal scallops in a warming oven.

3. Add lemon juice, parsley, capers, and dill to the skillet and heat for 1 minute, scraping browned bits off bottom.

4. Pour sauce over veal and serve, garnished with lemon slices.

Serves 4.

Calories per serving: 358
Preparation time: 2 minutes
Cooking time: 10 minutes

EMPRESS CHILI

Empress, or Cincinnati, chili is an elaborate concoction of ground beef and seasonings that has become a tradition in some midwestern cities. This version, however, contains about half the calories of the restaurant-style chili. Vary the spiciness of the recipe by increasing or decreasing the amounts of chili powder and cumin.

- 2 cups chopped onion
- 2 tablespoons minced garlic
- 1 cup chopped red bell pepper
- ¼ cup dry sherry
- 1 pound extralean ground beef
- 2 cups water
- 2 tablespoons apple cider vinegar
- 2 teaspoons Worcestershire sauce
- 3 tablespoons chili powder
- 1 tablespoon roasted carob powder
- 2 cups tomato sauce or stewed tomatoes
- 1 teaspoon cumin
- ¼ teaspoon allspice
- 1 teaspoon cinnamon
- ¼ teaspoon cayenne pepper
  Herbal salt substitute (optional)

1. In a large pot over medium heat, sauté onion, garlic, and bell pepper in sherry for 3 minutes.

2. Add remaining ingredients except salt substitute and bring to a boil. Lower heat, cover, and simmer for 1 hour, stirring occasionally.

3. Before serving, taste for seasoning and add salt substitute, if desired.

Serves 6.

Calories per serving: 281
Preparation time: 15 minutes
Cooking time: 75 minutes

HUNGARIAN BEEF PAPRIKASH

This simple stew recipe, cooked slowly in a heavy pot or Dutch oven, uses the delicate spices of paprika and caraway. Serve it with crusty French bread or roasted red potatoes, and a marinated cucumber salad.

- 1 pound lean beef, cubed
- 2 tablespoons flour
- 2 teaspoons paprika
- 1 teaspoon ground caraway seed
- 1 teaspoon herbal salt substitute
- ½ teaspoon freshly ground black pepper
- 1 teaspoon safflower oil
- 1½ cups sliced onion
- 1 cup sliced carrot
- ½ cup chopped red bell pepper
- 2 cloves garlic, minced
- 1 cup sliced button mushrooms
- ½ cup dry white wine
- ½ cup water
- 2 teaspoons tomato paste
- ¼ cup plain, nonfat yogurt

1. Trim fat from beef cubes. Combine flour, paprika, caraway, salt substitute, and pepper; dredge beef in seasoned flour.

2. In a deep, heavy pot heat oil and sauté onion, carrot, and bell pepper for 5 minutes over medium heat. Add garlic and mushrooms and continue cooking for 3 minutes. Shake excess flour from beef cubes and add beef to sauté. Cook 5 more minutes.

3. Add wine, water, and tomato paste. Cover pot tightly and cook over low heat for 1½ hours, stirring occasionally. Stir in yogurt before serving.

Serves 4.

Calories per serving: 403
Preparation time: 15 minutes
Cooking time: 2 hours

RAGOUT FIN

In this dainty veal dish, chopped veal is cooked lightly and then mixed with a mushroom cream sauce flavored with lemon juice, and baked with bread crumbs.

- 2 pounds veal
- 1 teaspoon herbal salt substitute
- ½ onion, chopped finely
- 1 cup water
- 1 teaspoon safflower oil
- 2 cups chopped mushrooms
- 2 teaspoons flour
  Juice of ½ lemon
- 2 teaspoons Worcestershire sauce, or to taste
- 1 egg yolk
- ½ cup fine bread crumbs

1. Preheat broiler. Cut veal into small pieces. Place in saucepan with salt substitute, onion, and the water. Bring to a boil and cook for 8 minutes. Drain veal from broth; reserve broth for later use.

2. In saucepan heat oil and sauté mushrooms over medium heat until they weep moisture. Add flour and cook, stirring, for 2 minutes. Slowly pour in ½ cup of reserved veal broth to thicken sauce. Add veal, lemon juice, and Worcestershire sauce.

3. Stir egg yolk into veal mixture. Spoon veal mixture into a baking dish. Top with bread crumbs.

4. Broil until lightly browned (about 1 minute).

Serves 6.

> *Calories per serving: 394*
> *Preparation time: 15 minutes*
> *Cooking time: 20 minutes*

Serve a piquant veal piccata for Sunday dinner; capers and lemon combine in the refreshing sauce. Accompany Veal With Lemon with steamed artichoke hearts and roasted new potatoes.

For your next grilling party try easy Marinated Beef Kabobs. The marinade combines the Middle Eastern flavors of curry, ginger, garlic, and chile with the tang of yogurt. Pair Marinated Beef Kabobs with grilled summer vegetables such as yellow crookneck squash, ripe tomatoes, and scallions.

MARINATED BEEF KABOBS

Lean chunks of beef are marinated in a tenderizing sauce of ginger, yogurt, and curry, and are then skewered and grilled. You can marinate the beef overnight, in a tightly covered container, and grill right before serving. Serve kabobs with a marinated tomato salad or coleslaw.

> 2 pounds lean beef, cubed
> 2 tablespoons grated fresh ginger
> 2 teaspoons herbal salt substitute
> 1 teaspoon hot chile oil
> 2 teaspoons curry powder
> 1 cup plain, nonfat yogurt
> 8 large cloves garlic, peeled and sliced thinly
> 4 cups cooked brown rice (optional)

1. Preheat broiler. Trim fat off beef cubes and place beef in a shallow bowl.

2. Mix ginger, salt substitute, oil, curry, and yogurt. Pour over beef. Let beef marinate for 24 hours. Stir occasionally.

3. Soak 12 bamboo skewers in salted water for 20 minutes.

4. Skewer beef cubes alternately with slices of garlic, pressing both together as tightly as possible on the skewers.

5. Broil kabobs for 5 minutes, turning to brown all sides. Serve over rice, if desired.

Serves 6.

> *Calories per serving: 444*
> *Preparation time: 15 minutes*
> *Marinating time: 24 hours*
> *Grilling time: 5 minutes*

LAMB ENTRÉES

Lamb is often a special treat because of its high price. Look for the more inexpensive cuts and tenderize them by marinating before cooking. Ground lamb, used in the following recipes, is also economical, and an excellent choice for a low-calorie recipe. Lamb needs fewer seasonings than beef and is tasty when mixed with mint, garlic, or nutmeg.

GREEK-STYLE LAMB MEATBALLS WITH MINT SAUCE

A Greek delicacy adapted for low-calorie cuisine, these lamb meatballs are cooked in a light tomato sauce with a hint of fresh mint. Serve them over steamed rice and wheat berries, or with a side of marinated cucumbers and sliced red onions. These meatballs can be made ahead and frozen, so they are ideal for entertaining.

> 1 cup minced onion
> 2 tablespoons minced shallot
> 1 pound lean ground lamb
> 1¼ cups finely ground bread crumbs
> ½ teaspoon ground nutmeg
> 2 teaspoons chopped fresh mint leaves
> 1 teaspoon herbal salt substitute
> ¼ teaspoon white pepper
> 2 cups tomato juice

1. Preheat oven to 350° F. Mix onion, shallot, and ground lamb. Form into 20 small balls.

2. Place remaining ingredients in a bowl and mix well.

3. Layer lamb meatballs in a shallow baking dish and pour tomato sauce mixture over them. Bake for 1 hour. Serve hot.

Makes 20 small meatballs, 4 servings.

> *Calories per serving: 478*
> *Preparation time: 40 minutes*
> *Cooking time: 1 hour*

TARABA
Spinach-wrapped lamb packets

Taraba is a traditional Mediterranean dish, similar in appearance to dolmas or stuffed grape leaves, except that spinach leaves are used to packet the small spiced balls of ground lamb. The mixture is then cooked in a tomato-lemon sauce. Make sure to choose large spinach leaves, so you can easily wrap the lamb mixture. You can secure with toothpicks, if necessary.

> 2 large bunches fresh spinach, washed and stemmed
> 2 pounds ground lamb
> ½ onion, minced
> 2 cloves garlic, minced
> Herbal salt substitute, to taste
> ¼ teaspoon cayenne pepper, or to taste
> 1 cup tomato sauce
> Juice of ½ lemon

1. Preheat oven to 350° F. Blanch spinach leaves briefly in boiling water. Drain and set aside.

2. Mix lamb, onion, garlic, salt substitute, and cayenne. Form into 20 small balls.

3. Wrap each lamb ball in a leaf of spinach. Place packets, seam side down, in a shallow baking dish.

4. Cover packets with tomato sauce and sprinkle with lemon juice. Bake until sauce is absorbed and packets are slightly browned (45 minutes to 1 hour).

Makes 18 small packets, 6 servings.

> *Calories per serving: 378*
> *Preparation time: 35 minutes*
> *Cooking time: 45 minutes–1 hour*

SIMPLE LOW-CALORIE SAUCES FOR CHICKEN AND LEAN MEATS

Most sauces use a high-calorie base of butter, cream, and meat fat, but they can be easily converted to low-calorie cooking. Wines add rich flavor without the calories of the above bases. You can also use a cooking method called reduction—where pan juices are cooked at high heat to evaporate the excess liquid and concentrate the flavors.

Wine sauces Heat a small amount of safflower oil or butter in a saucepan and add an equal amount of flour. Cook 2 minutes to form a thick paste. Pour in ½ to 1 cup of dry white or red wine, and cook until alcohol has cooked off and sauce is the thickness of heavy cream (about 5 minutes). Add to broiled beef, a chicken stir-fry, or roasted poultry.

Deglazing sauces Deglazing captures the rich flavor of wine and turns it into a sauce without adding fat. Once the poultry or meat is completely cooked, remove it to a platter and keep warm. Add directly to the pan juices in the roasting pan about the same amount of dry wine (use white for chicken- or fish-based sauce, red for beef, veal, or lamb) and bring to a boil. Boil rapidly at high heat until reduced to half of original volume.

En papillote sauces When cooking a piece of chicken or meat in parchment paper (*en papillote*), you can create a wonderful reduced sauce by using the juices from the cooking packet. Remove the portions of meat from the parchment before serving and place on a platter. Transfer the liquid from the packet to a saucepan and reduce by boiling rapidly for 5 minutes. Serve over the meat or chicken.

This elegant Far Eastern menu features a marinated cucumber salad, stir-fried chicken with Hunan spices, steamed asparagus, and poached whole peaches.

DINNER FROM THE FAR EAST

Salad of Sliced Cucumber and Red Onion

Hunan-Style Chicken Stir-fry With Vegetables

Boiled Chinese Rice Noodles

Steamed Asparagus With Lemon Juice

Poached Peaches in Orange Juice

Sparkling Water or Nonalcoholic White Wine

Entertain in the gracious style of the Orient. Warm sake or plum wine and serve in tiny glasses as an apéritif. Boil Chinese rice noodles, found in most Asian food stores, and then drain and reheat in boiling water for a few seconds before serving. Dress sliced cucumbers and red onions with a dash of rice vinegar and sesame oil. Steam asparagus just before serving. Menu serves six.

HUNAN-STYLE CHICKEN STIR-FRY WITH VEGETABLES

The only unusual ingredients in this spicy chicken dish are Chinese sesame paste, which is similar to Middle Eastern tahini, and Chinese chile paste with garlic. Both can be purchased at Asian markets, but substitutes are also listed in the ingredients list.

> 1 teaspoon safflower oil
> ⅓ cup sliced green onion
> ⅓ cup diagonally sliced carrot
> ⅓ cup sliced red bell pepper
> ⅓ cup broccoli florets
> ¼ cup dry sherry or rice wine
> 2 cups shredded cooked chicken breast, skinned
> 1 teaspoon dark sesame oil
> 2 teaspoons minced garlic
> 2 teaspoons Chinese sesame paste or peanut butter
> 1 tablespoon rice vinegar
> 2 tablespoons low-sodium tamari or soy sauce
> 1 teaspoon honey
> 1 tablespoon Chinese chile paste with garlic or ¼ teaspoon cayenne pepper
> 2 teaspoons grated fresh ginger

1. In a wok or skillet, heat safflower oil and sauté green onion until soft but not browned. Add carrot, bell pepper, broccoli, and sherry. Cook rapidly over high heat, covered, for 3 minutes.

2. Add chicken, sesame oil, garlic, sesame paste, rice vinegar, tamari, honey, chile paste, and ginger. Lower heat and cook, covered, for 5 minutes, stirring frequently. Serve hot.

Serves 6.

> *Calories per serving: 94*
> *Preparation time: 25 minutes*
> *Cooking time: 15 minutes*

POACHED PEACHES IN ORANGE JUICE

This simple yet luscious dessert calls for fresh peaches, but you can substitute apples, pears, or the exotic Asian pear that is available in some markets. Left to chill in its syrup, the fruit absorbs flavor and remains moist until ready to serve to guests. A suitable ending to an Asian meal, the orange juice sauce has a slight tang of cinnamon that blends well with Chinese cuisine.

> 6 large peaches, slightly underripe
> 6 tablespoons grated orange rind
> 1 tablespoon cinnamon
> ¼ cup honey
> 2 tablespoons maple syrup
> Juice of 6 oranges

1. Preheat oven to 350° F. With a sharp knife, cut the top off each peach about ⅓ of the way down. Wiggling it slightly with your fingers, remove the pit. Place peaches in a deep baking dish.

2. Mix remaining ingredients and fill the cavity of each peach, then pour the remaining sauce around the peaches as a poaching liquid. Replace peach tops.

3. Bake until peaches are the softness of canned fruit (about 25 minutes). Chill for 1 hour, and serve with extra poaching liquid as a sauce.

Serves 6.

> *Calories per serving: 161*
> *Preparation time: 10 minutes*
> *Cooking time: 25 minutes*
> *Chilling time: 1 hour*

Flavor, nutritional value, and low calories are the benefits of fish and shellfish purchased fresh from the market.

Fish & Shellfish

Researchers have found that a diet containing plenty of seafood can keep us healthy in many ways (see page 99). Yet cooking fish can be a tricky business. This chapter gives step-by-step instructions for preparing fish and shellfish that will delight your palate as well as shrink your waistline. You can prepare an elegant seafood entrée, such as Baked Salmon Niçoise (see page 88), a flavorful fish soup, such as Crab Bisque (see page 97), or a light and easy Seafood Salad (see page 99). The busy cook will be pleased with tips for preparing a wide variety of low-calorie sauces (see page 91) and freezing fish (see page 96). The chapter ends with an Island Buffet (see page 100), featuring Mahi-mahi With Lemon and Pineapple Salsa.

INTERNATIONAL FISH ENTRÉES

The following recipes have an international flair and are delectable enough for any type of entertaining. Considering that most fish dishes don't hold their fresh flavor and texture if prepared too far in advance, they usually must be cooked right before serving, so it helps if accompanying dishes are simple, make-ahead recipes.

JAMAICAN ESCOVEICH FISH

You'll find in this recipe many of the subtle seasonings of the island of Jamaica. Fish steaks (such as swordfish, salmon, or shark) are simmered with green onions, red bell pepper, tomatoes, and spices. Traditionally this dish is served with cooked rice or crusty bread.

    4 fish steaks
    2 teaspoons olive oil
    1 bunch green onions
        (including greens), chopped
    2 large tomatoes, chopped
    1 red bell pepper, seeded and
        chopped
    1 teaspoon herbal salt substitute
    ½ teaspoon freshly ground
        black pepper
    ¼ cup white wine vinegar
    ½ teaspoon dried thyme
    1 tablespoon honey

1. Wash fish steaks and pat dry with paper towels. Carefully remove and discard any bones you find.

2. In a skillet heat oil; add fish and brown quickly on both sides at high heat. Add green onions, tomatoes, and bell pepper. Cover and cook 5 minutes.

3. Add remaining ingredients and continue cooking, covered, for 15 more minutes. Serve immediately.

Serves 4.

> *Calories per serving: 288*
> *Preparation time: 20 minutes*
> *Cooking time: 30 minutes*

BAKED SALMON NIÇOISE

Similar to Chicken Niçoise (see page 73), Baked Salmon Niçoise combines the subtle flavors of several Mediterranean cuisines. Small fillets of salmon are baked in parchment paper in order to retain moistness and soft texture. Prepare the packets ahead of time, refrigerate, and pull out to bake just before serving. You can use any firm-fleshed fish in season, such as tuna or cod, if salmon is not available.

    1 teaspoon olive oil
    3 cloves garlic, minced
    1 cup chopped plum tomatoes
    ¼ cup chopped pitted Italian or
        Greek olives
    ¼ cup minced green bell pepper
    ¼ teaspoon saffron threads
    ½ teaspoon dried tarragon
    ¼ teaspoon dried thyme
        Pinch dried sage
    1¼ cups white wine
    4 salmon fillets or small
        salmon steaks

1. Preheat oven to 350° F. In a large, heavy skillet heat olive oil and sauté garlic, tomatoes, olives, and bell pepper until soft.

2. Add saffron threads, tarragon, thyme, sage, and wine. Cook 5 minutes at medium heat, uncovered.

3. Place each portion of salmon on a parchment sheet. Spoon tomato mixture over fish and fold packets to seal. Place on a baking sheet.

4. Bake salmon packets for 10 minutes. Slit the top of each packet before serving.

Serves 4.

> *Calories per serving: 368*
> *Preparation time: 30 minutes*
> *Cooking time: 10 minutes*

INDONESIAN CRAB CURRY

Indonesian curries are often made with coconut milk, a thick liquid pressed from the pulp of the coconut after it is blended with water. To lower the calories of this usually rich dish, nonfat milk is mixed with coconut milk to create a thick sauce. Serve with small garnishes of chopped dried fruits, fresh cilantro, and lime slices.

    1½ teaspoons cayenne pepper
    1 teaspoon grated fresh ginger
    ½ teaspoon freshly ground
        black pepper
    4 cloves garlic, minced
    5 shallots, minced
    ⅓ cup chopped fresh coriander
        (including stems, leaves, and
        roots)
    ½ teaspoon grated lime rind
    ½ teaspoon herbal salt substitute
    1 teaspoon dried shrimp paste
        (optional; see Note)
    ½ cup grated coconut
    2 cups nonfat milk
    2 tablespoons Thai fish sauce
        (see Note) or low-sodium
        tamari or soy sauce
    1 tablespoon honey
    1 pound cooked crabmeat
    5 cups cooked brown rice

1. In a stockpot combine cayenne, ginger, pepper, garlic, shallots, coriander, lime rind, salt substitute, shrimp paste (if used), coconut, and milk. Bring to a boil and cook over medium high heat for 10 minutes.

2. Add fish sauce, honey, and crabmeat. Heat through. Serve hot over rice.

Serves 6.

<u>Note</u> You can buy shrimp paste and Thai fish sauce in most Asian food stores.

> *Calories per serving: 336*
> *Preparation time: 15 minutes*
> *Cooking time: 20 minutes*

FENNEL BAKED FISH EN PAPILLOTE

En papillote is a French cooking term that refers to parchment baking. In this recipe small portions of fresh fish are lightly seasoned with fennel, garlic, and cayenne pepper and then wrapped in parchment packets and baked. This method of cooking fish is excellent for retaining flavor and juiciness.

        2   *whole trout, boned*
        2   *teaspoons ground fennel seed*
        1   *large clove garlic, minced*
        ¼   *teaspoon herbal salt substitute*
            Pinch cayenne pepper
        ¼   *teaspoon freshly ground*
            black pepper
        2   *teaspoons butter*
            Juice of 1 lemon

1. Preheat oven to 450° F. Place each trout on a piece of parchment paper.

2. Mix fennel, garlic, salt substitute, cayenne, pepper, butter, and lemon juice to a thick paste. Spread half of paste inside each trout. Wrap the edges of the parchment up around the fish, forming a loose packet.

3. Place packets on a baking sheet and bake for 12 minutes. To serve, open packets and remove trout, reserving cooking liquid. Cut each trout into 2 fillets. Place 1 fillet on each person's plate and top with cooking liquid.

Serves 4.

> *Calories per serving: 85*
> *Preparation time: 20 minutes*
> *Cooking time: 12 minutes*

Pungent garlic, ginger, and cayenne flavor this exotic yet easy to prepare Indonesian Crab Curry.

*A delicate French salad,
Coquilles Sauce Verte
combines wine-poached
scallops with a low-calorie
dill and mayonnaise
sauce. Traditionally it
is served chilled on a bed
of crisp greens.*

COQUILLES SAUCE VERTE
Scallops in green sauce

A traditional French salad, often
served as a small, delicate appetizer,
this fresh scallop dish is poached
in white wine, and then mixed with
a light dressing. Serve it chilled on
lettuce leaves with a garnish of
minced parsley.

> 1 *pound bay scallops*
> ¾ *cup dry white wine*
> ¼ *onion, minced*
> ⅓ *cup low-calorie mayonnaise*
> ¼ *cup minced parsley, plus
>   parsley for garnish*
> ⅓ *cup chopped spinach leaves*
> ¼ *cup minced green onion*
> ¼ *teaspoon dill*
> 6 *lettuce leaves, for lining plates*

1. Place scallops, wine, and onion in
a saucepan and bring to a boil,
uncovered. Cook 1 minute. Drain
scallops and refrigerate immediately
to stop cooking process. Discard
cooking liquid, or save as fish stock
for another recipe.

2. In a blender purée mayonnaise,
parsley, spinach, green onion, and
dill until smooth.

3. Toss chilled scallops with puréed
green sauce. Chill for 10 minutes,
then serve on lettuce leaves. Garnish
with additional minced parsley, if
desired.

Serves 6.

*Calories per serving: 138
Preparation time: 20 minutes*

MEXICAN BAKED FISH IN SALSA VERDE

This parchment-packeted fish is baked in a green hot sauce made from tomatillos and green chiles. Both of these Mexican items are available canned (wash off any pickling marinade before using in this recipe). You can prepare the packets ahead of time, wrap well, and refrigerate until cooking time.

> 1½ pounds fresh salmon, cod, or red snapper, cut into 1-inch-thick fillets
> 1 teaspoon olive oil
> ¼ cup dry white wine
> 1 cup chopped onion
> ⅓ cup chopped green bell pepper
> 1 clove garlic, minced
> 1 cup chopped fresh tomatillos
> 1 teaspoon cumin
> 2 tablespoons chopped chiles en escabeche (marinated chiles)
> 1 teaspoon each lemon juice and lime juice
> ⅓ cup chopped cilantro

1. Preheat oven to 475° F. Cut fish fillets into 4 servings. Carefully remove bones. Place each portion on top of a sheet of parchment paper.

2. In a skillet heat oil and wine; add onion and sauté until soft. Add bell pepper, garlic, tomatillos, and cumin. Continue cooking for 8 minutes.

3. Add remaining ingredients and cook 3 more minutes.

4. Spoon sautéed vegetables over portions of fish. Wrap parchment into envelopes, sealing fish completely. Place on a baking sheet.

5. Bake parchment packets for 10 minutes. Serve by cutting packets down the center and placing on a platter or on individual plates.

Serves 4.

> *Calories per serving: 384*
> *Preparation time: 15 minutes*
> *Cooking time: 20 minutes*

SICILIAN SEAFOOD BROCHETTES

Sicilian cooking has much in common with that of southern Italy: Olive oil, seafood, and red peppers are used abundantly. These delicious, grilled brochettes are made from skewered pieces of fresh snapper, large scallops, and shelled prawns, alternated with fresh vegetables. Requiring short preparation time, these brochettes make a perfect summer meal. Assemble them early in the day, wrap tightly in plastic wrap, refrigerate, and then grill right before dinner.

> 2 small red snapper or cod fillets
> 1 red bell pepper
> 8 large scallops
> 8 medium prawns, shelled and deveined
> 8 small boiling onions
> 4 small new potatoes, cooked whole
> 2 teaspoons olive oil

1. Preheat broiler. Soak 8 bamboo skewers in salted water for 20 minutes to prevent burning on the grill (use about 2 tablespoons of salt to 2 cups of water).

2. Cut snapper into 2-inch squares. Cut bell pepper into cubes.

3. Skewer fish and shellfish alternately with onions, bell peppers, and potatoes. Brush lightly with olive oil.

4. Grill until prawns turn pink and curl slightly (5 to 10 minutes). Serve immediately.

Serves 4.

> *Calories per serving: 354*
> *Preparation time: 20 minutes*
> *Cooking time: 10 minutes*

Basics

SIMPLE LOW-CALORIE SAUCES FOR FISH AND SEAFOOD

Acidic sauces Fish responds very well to a slightly acidic sauce, which subdues the fishy flavor and enhances the sweetness. Try lemon or lime juice-based sauces that are thickened with a little arrowroot slurry and seasoned with herbs and freshly ground pepper. To make a slurry, mix equal amounts of arrowroot powder and cold water; heat until slightly thickened. Use about 2 tablespoons of slurry for every 1 cup of sauce you want to thicken.

Wine sauces These sauces are great on fish, especially if you choose a light dry wine, such as a California Chardonnay. Heat wine to boiling, add fresh or dried herbs—such as tarragon, dill, or chives—and reduce over medium high heat for 10 minutes. Poach fish in this mixture, or dribble it over fish in parchment packets, then bake.

Fruit juice sauces Try grilling fish with freshly squeezed fruit juices. Use orange, grapefruit, or lemon juices, seasoned with hot chile oil or a dash of cayenne pepper. Marinate fillets or steaks of salmon or tuna in the mixture, and then grill, basting with the marinade every few minutes.

Herb sauces As the fish poaches or bakes, baste with an herb paste made from pressed garlic, minced shallots or onions, and lemon juice. Or try stuffing the inside cavity of a whole fish, such as trout, with this mixture.

JAPANESE BAKED FISH

The Asian-style sauce in this recipe uses Japanese miso, a fermented paste made from soybeans, one of the best sources of protein. Miso paste, with a taste similar to peanut butter, is found refrigerated in Asian markets and health food stores. The light (yellow) miso used in this recipe is milder than dark (red) miso and combines well with ginger and sake, which are both used in this fish dish. You can make the miso-sesame sauce ahead of time and spread it on the fillets right before baking. See Cutting Fish Fillets and Steaks on opposite page if you are cutting your own fillets.

- 2 pounds red snapper or cod, cut into 4 portions
- 2 tablespoons toasted sesame seed
- 1 teaspoon grated fresh ginger
- 2 tablespoons light-colored miso paste
- 1 teaspoon maple syrup or honey
- 1 tablespoon sake
- 2 tablespoons dry sherry
- 3 tablespoons lemon juice
- 1 teaspoon dark sesame oil

1. Preheat oven to 450° F. Place snapper fillets in a large baking dish.

2. In a bowl combine other ingredients. Spread miso mixture evenly over fillets and bake for 12 minutes. Serve at once.

Serves 4.

Calories per serving: 319 *Preparation time: 15 minutes* *Cooking time: 12 minutes*

SWEET-AND-SOUR PRAWNS OVER ALMOND RICE

It's a good idea to slightly undercook the prawns in this recipe since they will continue cooking in the hot sauce even when removed from heat. Almond Rice has a crunchy texture and complements the prawns. Make the rice ahead, but cook the prawns right before serving for best flavor.

- 1 pound medium prawns, shelled and deveined
- 1 cup pineapple chunks
- 1 red bell pepper, seeded and cut into strips
- 1 head broccoli, cut into florets
- ¼ cup dry sherry
- ½ cup rice vinegar
- 4 tablespoons low-sodium tamari or soy sauce
- ¼ cup honey
- 2 teaspoons dark sesame oil
- 1 large clove garlic, minced
- 1 tablespoon arrowroot powder mixed with 2 tablespoons cold water

Almond Rice

- 2 tablespoons slivered almonds
- 1 teaspoon light sesame oil
- ⅓ cup chopped green onion
- 4 cups cooked brown rice

1. Cut each prawn into bite-sized chunks. Place in a wok or deep skillet with pineapple, bell pepper, broccoli, and sherry. Sauté until prawns turn bright pink (about 5 minutes).

2. Combine remaining ingredients in a small bowl and add to sauté. Cook, stirring, over medium-high heat until sauce thickens.

3. Prepare Almond Rice. Serve sweet-and-sour prawns and vegetables over heated rice.

Serves 6.

Almond Rice In a small pan sauté almonds at medium-high heat in light sesame oil for 1 minute, stirring frequently. Add green onion and rice. Heat through.

Calories per serving: 433 *Preparation time: 20 minutes* *Cooking time: 15 minutes*

STEAMED FISH WITH GINGER

This is a good recipe for light, flat fish, such as sole or flounder. Steaming is a very fast method of preparing fish and should be done right before serving. Be sure that your cover fits snugly over the steamer basket. The light ginger sauce complements the firm texture of the fish.

- 4 sole fillets (approximately 6 to 8 oz each)
- ½ cup boiling water
- ½ cup white wine
- 2 tablespoons grated fresh ginger
- 2 cloves garlic, minced
- 2 teaspoons dark sesame oil
- 1 teaspoon arrowroot powder mixed with 2 tablespoons cold water
- 1 teaspoon low-sodium tamari or soy sauce

1. Place fillets on a steamer basket large enough to fit snugly inside a deep skillet. Pour water and wine into the skillet and bring to a boil. Set the steamer basket in the skillet and cover. Steam 3 minutes.

2. While fish is steaming, sauté ginger and garlic in sesame oil for 3 minutes. Add arrowroot mixture and tamari. Continue cooking until sauce thickens, stirring frequently.

3. To serve, ladle a small amount of sauce over each fillet of steamed fish.

Serves 4.

Note Steam can cause severe burns. When you lift the cover from your steamer basket, open it away from you and let the steam dissipate before reaching or looking inside.

Calories per serving: 211 *Preparation time: 15 minutes* *Cooking time: 10 minutes*

CUTTING FISH FILLETS AND STEAKS

The most important factor in choosing fish is freshness. A truly fresh fish should not smell fishy; a fishy smell is a sign of age or improper handling by the fishmonger. A fresh fish has a mild odor; firm, elastic flesh that springs back when pressed; clear, protruding eyes; reddish or pink gills; and scales that are shiny, bright and tight to the skin.

When buying steaks or fillets look for flesh with a natural sheen that is free from yellowing or browning around the edges. If the fish has been frozen, ask how long it has been defrosted. Do not buy anything that has been defrosted for more than two days. It is better to purchase frozen fish and defrost it at home. For best quality, try to find fish that were individually quick-frozen on the fishing vessel.

Fish may be categorized as either lean or oily. Lean fish have a mild flavor and firm white flesh and contain 5 percent or less fat. Take care in applying dry-heat cooking process to lean fish; they dry out easily. Examples of lean fish include sole, flounder, turbot, cod, pollack, sea bass, rockfish, snapper, drum, bass, and burbot.

Oily fish contain 5 to 50 percent fat. They usually have flesh that is richer and stronger, and have less white flesh than do lean fish. The fat is distributed throughout the flesh, which helps keep the fish moist during cooking. Examples of oily fish are swordfish, smelt, salmon, bluefish, tuna, mullet, mackerel, trout, catfish, sablefish, sturgeon, and pompano.

Steaks are cross-sections cut from a whole fish. Fillets are long pieces of boneless fish. Roundfish and flatfish require slightly different filleting techniques.

To Fillet a Roundfish

1. *Make a slit along backbone from head to tail.*

2. *Next, make a cut behind gill. Holding head, insert knife between fillet and ribs. Sliding knife along ribs, cut down the length of the fillet. Pull fillet free and sever skin at the anal fin. Repeat the filleting process on the other side of the fish.*

To Skin a Fillet

To skin a fillet, place it skin side down and cut a small section of flesh away from the skin close to the tail. Hold knife at a 15-degree angle to the cutting board. Holding skin taut, scrape the knife along the skin without cutting it.

To Fillet a Flatfish

1. *Place the skinned flatfish on a board with the eyes up. Cut through the flesh to the backbone (which is in the middle of the fish) from head to tail. Insert the knife blade at a shallow angle between the ribs and the end of the fillet close to the head. Cut down the length of a fillet on one side of the backbone and remove it.*

2. *Cut the remaining top fillet using the same technique. Turn the fish over. Remove the two bottom fillets.*

To Cut a Steak

Using a large, sharp knife, cut off the head just behind gills. Slice the fish into steaks of the desired thickness, usually between 1 and 1½ inches.

FISH SOUPS, STEWS, AND ONE-DISH MEALS

Another way to cut back on calories is to have your entire meal in one bowl. The following recipes are winners for the busy cook: They can be made ahead in quantity and even frozen. Use them when entertaining by simply serving with a tossed salad, French bread, and a fruit dessert.

ITALIAN FISH SOUP

This recipe is a tradition on the island of Sicily, where the catch of the day is cooked each night in a large pot with savory spices, tomatoes, and olive oil. You can make this recipe ahead of time; it freezes well and will keep in the refrigerator for up to six days. Serve with crusty French bread, a green salad, and then a light fruit dessert.

- 1 teaspoon olive oil
- ¼ cup dry sherry
- ½ cup sliced onion
- ⅓ cup diced carrot
- 2½ cups crushed tomato (canned or fresh)
- 2 cups red potatoes, diced
- ⅛ teaspoon crushed red chile
- 1 cup water
- 1 teaspoon fresh basil, minced
- 6 tablespoons chopped parsley
- 1 pound white fish (such as cod), cut into 1-inch pieces
  Herbal salt substitute and ground black pepper, if needed

1. In a large stockpot heat oil and sherry and sauté onion over medium-high heat until soft but not browned. Add carrot and tomato and continue cooking for 5 minutes.

2. Add potatoes, chile, water, basil, parsley, and fish and bring to a boil. Lower heat, cover, and simmer until potatoes are soft (about 20 minutes).

3. Add salt substitute and pepper, if needed, and serve hot.

Serves 6.

> *Calories per serving: 121*
> *Preparation time: 25 minutes*
> *Cooking time: 35 minutes*

BASQUE PAELLA

This dish takes a bit of extra time to prepare but is well worth the effort. A beautiful medley of saffron rice, red and green bell peppers, and cooked shellfish, it is served as a one-pot meal. Paella is a traditional Spanish dish, and this version incorporates some of the pronounced seasonings of the Basque area of Spain.

- 1 teaspoon olive oil
- 2 teaspoons safflower oil
- 1 cup boned and skinned white meat of chicken, sliced
- 1 cup uncooked basmati rice
- 2 cups boiling water
- ½ cup chopped onion
- 2 cloves garlic, minced
- ½ cup each sliced red bell pepper and sliced green bell pepper
- ½ cup diced tomato
- 1 red snapper fillet, cut into 1-inch pieces
- 2 cups hot, defatted Chicken Stock (see page 31)
- 1 tablespoon herbal salt substitute
- 1 teaspoon saffron threads
- ¾ teaspoon oregano
- 6 large prawns, shelled and deveined
- 1 cup peas, fresh or frozen
- 5 artichoke hearts, unmarinated
- 6 clams in their shells (scrub outside of shells)

1. In large, heavy skillet over medium-high heat, combine oils and cook chicken pieces until just opaque. Remove chicken to platter. Reserve skillet.

2. Soak rice in the boiling water for 10 minutes, then drain.

3. In reserved skillet sauté onion over medium heat until soft (about 5 minutes). Add garlic, bell peppers, and tomato and continue sautéing for 5 more minutes.

4. Add snapper, soaked rice with water, stock, salt substitute, saffron, and oregano. Bring to a boil, then lower heat to medium. Cover pot and let simmer until rice is tender and has absorbed liquid (about 15 minutes).

5. Arrange prawns, peas, artichoke hearts, cooked chicken pieces, and clams on top of rice. Cover and cook again until prawns turn bright pink and clam shells open (about 10 minutes). Serve hot.

Serves 8.

> *Calories per serving: 221*
> *Preparation time: 35 minutes*
> *Cooking time: 45 minutes*

COUSIN LOU'S LOUISIANA CREOLE

An original recipe from Crowley, Louisiana, this shrimp Creole is an easy, satisfying one-pot meal. Use fresh vegetables that liven up the dish with greens and reds. This Creole dish can be frozen and reheated for later use, or refrigerated in a tightly covered container for up to five days.

- 1 teaspoon olive oil
- ½ onion, chopped coarsely
- 4 cloves garlic, minced
- 6 Spanish green olives, pitted and chopped
- 1½ cup peeled, chopped tomato
- 1 green bell pepper, chopped
- ½ bay leaf
- ¼ teaspoon dried thyme
- 1 teaspoon dried parsley
- 1 teaspoon honey
- ½ teaspoon cayenne pepper, or to taste
- 1 teaspoon herbal salt substitute
- 1 pound peeled and deveined medium prawns
- 3 cups cooked brown rice

1. In a heavy pot or Dutch oven, heat oil and sauté onion over medium heat until golden brown. Add garlic, olives, tomato, and bell pepper. Sauté 2 minutes more.

2. Add bay leaf, thyme, parsley, honey, cayenne, and salt substitute. Let mixture simmer over low heat, covered, for 20 minutes.

3. Add prawns. Cook until they turn bright pink. Serve over hot rice.

Serves 4.

> *Calories per serving: 346*
> *Preparation time: 20 minutes*
> *Cooking time: 40 minutes*

Flavors of Spain enrich this Basque Paella of herbed saffron rice, artichoke hearts, red and green peppers, prawns, clams, chicken, and white fish.

... ON FREEZING FISH

The old saying, "The greatest enemies of fish are not fishermen, but cooks," still holds true today. Many cooks don't know how to store or prepare fish to retain the delicate textures and flavors.

Freshly caught fish is a melt-in-your-mouth experience. Frozen fish can be almost as good, if care is taken in the storage process. Modern supermarkets freeze fish in vacuum-sealed plastic bags—a process that keeps much of the flavor intact. Here are some tips for freezing fresh fish at home.

☐ Years ago it was common to freeze fish in milk. This may sound strange today, but it is an excellent way to keep fish from developing a strong flavor or becoming freezer burned. Save milk cartons for this type of storage. Place the fish in a plastic bag, seal it tightly to remove as much air as possible, put it in the milk carton, and fill carton three fourths full with milk so that it surrounds the sealed bag.

☐ To defrost fish, let it thaw overnight in the refrigerator. Quick defrosting, such as in hot water or even at room temperature, can destroy much of the delicate flavor of fish.

☐ Fish is best when it is not frozen longer than three months.

☐ It is usually better to prepare a dish while the fish is fresh, and then to freeze the completed soup or stew after it has cooked. The other ingredients in the recipe help the fish retain more moisture and flavor.

HALIBUT WITH APPLES AND HORSERADISH

This unusual Russian dish combines the tartness of horseradish with the sweetness of cooked, puréed apples. The fish is tenderized and sweetened by a vinegar-onion broth. You can prepare the ingredients for this dish beforehand, but cook the fish right before serving for best results.

2 pounds halibut or cod
1 cup white wine vinegar or apple cider vinegar
½ cup sliced leek
1½ cups sliced onion
½ teaspoon dried thyme
¼ cup minced parsley
½ teaspoon freshly ground pepper

Russian Applesauce

1 cup sliced tart apples
1 tablespoon honey
¼ cup apple juice
1 teaspoon lemon juice
¼ cup freshly grated horseradish root or prepared horseradish, drained

1. Cut fish into 4 fillets. Remove and discard any bones. Place fish in a large saucepan.

2. Cover fish with vinegar, leek, onion, thyme, parsley, and pepper. Bring to a boil and cook over medium heat, uncovered, until fish is fork tender (about 8 minutes). Prepare sauce while fish is cooking.

3. Serve fish and vegetables topped with apple mixture.

Serves 4.

Russian Applesauce In a saucepan mix apples, honey, apple juice, and lemon juice. Bring to a boil and cook over high heat, covered, for 5 minutes. Mash apples with a fork. Stir in horseradish and mix well.

Calories per serving: 250
Preparation time: 25 minutes
Cooking time: 25 minutes

LIGHT AND EASY SEAFOODS

The recipes that follow are particularly suited to light meals, such as a summer luncheon, an after-theater gathering, or an hors d'oeuvre at your next dinner party. They are ideal for entertaining since most can be made ahead and chilled or reheated just before serving.

SAUTÉED SALMON FILLETS WITH RED PEPPER

This delicate entrée visually dazzles—bright pink salmon fillets are braised in a marinade of light rice wine and sesame oil, and are then garnished with sautéed strips of sweet red and green bell peppers.

1 medium-sized salmon fillet
¼ cup dark sesame oil
⅓ cup rice wine
2 teaspoons minced garlic
¼ cup dry sherry
1 large red bell pepper, julienned
1 large green bell pepper, julienned

1. Place salmon fillets in a shallow pan. In a separate bowl mix sesame oil, rice wine, and garlic; spread mixture over fillets. Let marinate for 30 minutes.

2. In a large skillet heat sherry and add bell peppers. Stir well and cook over medium heat for 5 minutes. Set aside.

3. Preheat broiler. Broil salmon until flesh begins to flake when pressed with a fork (5 to 8 minutes). Add sautéed bell peppers during last 2 minutes of cooking. Serve hot.

Serves 4.

Calories per serving: 303
Preparation time: 10 minutes
Marinating time: 30 minutes
Cooking time: 10–13 minutes

CRAB BISQUE

Originally bisque was a very rich, cream-based soup. This bisque is thickened with cooked potatoes instead of butter and cream.

2 teaspoons butter
2 cups coarsely chopped onion
⅓ cup chopped celery (including leaves)
2 large russet potatoes, peeled and cubed
2 cups Fish Stock (see page 31) or clam juice
2 tablespoons tomato paste
⅔ cup dry sherry
2 cups nonfat milk
½ pound cooked fresh crabmeat
 Herbal salt substitute and pepper, to taste
 Minced parsley, for garnish

1. In a large stockpot heat butter and sauté onion and celery over medium-high heat until onion and celery are soft but not browned.

2. Add potato and fish stock. Bring to a boil. Lower heat, cover, and simmer until potato is soft (about 20 minutes).

3. Add tomato paste, sherry, and milk. Continue cooking 10 more minutes.

4. Purée mixture in blender. Return to stockpot and add crabmeat. Heat through. Taste for seasoning; add salt substitute and pepper as needed. Serve garnished with minced parsley.

Serves 6.

Calories per serving: 188
Preparation time: 15 minutes
Cooking time: 40 minutes

A rich yet low-calorie soup, this creamy bisque is made with fresh crabmeat, sherry, and tomato paste, and thickened with potato purée. Serve Crab Bisque, which can be made ahead and frozen, with a spinach or tossed salad and crusty brown bread for a delicious lunch.

An easy appetizer for entertaining or a great summer luncheon, these avocado shells are filled with a surprisingly low-calorie mixture of chile, celery, shrimp, lime juice, and low-calorie mayonnaise. A bed of burgundy-colored radicchio lines the platter.

SALMON MOUSSE

Serve this delicate mousse as a spread on open sandwiches—just add chopped green onions, parsley, and endive. Or try it as an appetizer on melba toasts or celery boats. It keeps for five to six days in a tightly covered container in the refrigerator.

The poaching of the salmon in this recipe should be done over low heat to prevent the outside of the fish from cooking before the inside and to prevent the fish from falling apart.

> 1 package unflavored gelatin
> 3 tablespoons cold water
> 8 ounces salmon fillet or drained canned salmon
> ½ cup white wine (optional)
> ½ cup nonfat, plain yogurt
> ½ cup farmer cheese
> 2 tablespoons chives, preferably fresh
> 2 teaspoons lemon juice
> 2 teaspoons herbal salt substitute, or to taste
> Freshly ground pepper, to taste
> Oil, for greasing mold

1. In a saucepan dissolve gelatin in the cold water. Place in a saucepan and cook over low heat, stirring, until gelatin is completely dissolved. Let cool while fresh salmon is poached.

2. If using fresh salmon, place in a skillet or saucepan with white wine and bring to a boil. Cook until salmon flakes and turns dull pink. (If salmon is canned, omit this step.)

3. Drain salmon. Place salmon, gelatin, yogurt, cheese, chives, lemon juice, salt substitute, and pepper in a blender or food processor and purée until smooth.

4. Lightly oil a decorative mold and spoon in salmon mousse. Chill until set (about 25 minutes).

5. Unmold by dipping the outside of the mold in very hot tap water and turning carefully onto a plate.

Serves 8.

Calories per serving: 83
Preparation time: 15 minutes
Chilling time: 25 minutes

SEAFOOD SALAD

Here's an easy recipe that can be prepared two hours before serving, wrapped tightly in plastic wrap, and chilled. Serve on lettuce leaves, and garnish with raw vegetables, such as red bell pepper strips, endive spears, and cherry tomatoes. Use whatever fish is fresh and in season, but make sure that it is firm and can be poached without losing its shape.

> 1 pound fish fillets (such as tuna or salmon)
> ¼ pound prawns, shelled and deveined
> 1 cup white wine
> ¾ cup diced celery
> 1 teaspoon minced fresh tarragon
> 2 green onions (including greens), chopped
> ⅓ cup low-calorie mayonnaise
> 1 teaspoon herbal salt substitute
> 2 teaspoons low-sodium tamari or soy sauce
> 1 teaspoon Dijon mustard
> 1 tablespoon plain, nonfat yogurt
> Lettuce leaves, for lining serving bowl

1. Place fish and prawns in a small saucepan and pour in wine. Heat to boiling and poach until prawns turn bright pink (about 8 minutes). Drain and let cool. Cut fish and prawns into bite-sized pieces.

2. In a small bowl mix remaining ingredients except lettuce and toss with cooked fish and prawns.

3. Line a serving bowl or platter with lettuce leaves and spoon seafood into the center. Serve at room temperature, or chill if desired.

Serves 4 to 6.

> *Calories per serving: 174*
> *Preparation time: 20 minutes*
> *Cooking time: 15 minutes*

AVOCADO SHELLS STUFFED WITH SHRIMP

With their relatively high fat content, avocados are usually considered a food to avoid when trying to lose or maintain weight, but you can eat a small amount without worrying. In this recipe avocado is mixed with seasonings and cooked shrimp and spooned into avocado shells. The bright green of the avocado and the pink of the shrimp make a colorful combination. Prepare this recipe just before serving for best color and flavor.

> 2 avocados (preferably Hass black-skinned)
> ½ pound cooked shrimp meat
> 2 chiles en escabeche (marinated chiles)
> 3 tablespoons low-calorie mayonnaise
> ⅓ cup diced celery
> 2 teaspoons minced onion
> 2 teaspoons herbal salt substitute
> Juice of ½ lime
> Radicchio leaves, for lining platter

1. Cut avocados in half, remove pit, scoop out pulp. Reserve shells. Mash ½ cup of pulp and reserve remainder for another use.

2. In a large bowl combine pulp with remaining ingredients.

3. Stuff avocado mixture into avocado shells and arrange on radicchio-lined platter. Chill slightly and serve.

Serves 4.

> *Calories per serving: 176*
> *Preparation time: 20 minutes*

TAKE FISH TO HEART

Researchers recently found an interesting correlation between prevention of heart disease and certain fish oils, called omega-3 long-chain fatty acids. One study discovered that Greenland Eskimos, whose diet is loaded with fish, have very low rates of heart disease. It's believed that fish oils can help lower blood cholesterol and reduce the tendency of the blood to form clots. Fish with high omega-3 oils include tuna, salmon, trout, sardines, mackerel, swordfish, and herring. Squid and low-cholesterol shellfish—such as mussels, oysters, and scallops—also contain high amounts of omega-3 oils.

Most types of seafood are relatively low in cholesterol. New, sophisticated testing methods, in fact, show that certain seafood has less cholesterol than previously believed. Seafood is also relatively low in calories (as long as not served with creamy sauces or butter).

The following chart lists the most recent calorie and cholesterol counts for a few popular shellfish. Note the relatively high cholesterol level of shrimp, crayfish, and particularly squid (calamari), which has almost as much cholesterol as eggs.

	Calories*	Cholesterol
Abalone	105	85 mg
Clams	75	34 mg
Crab, Dungeness	85	59 mg
Crab, king	85	42 mg
Crayfish	85	139 mg
Lobster	90	80 mg
Mussels	85	28 mg
Oysters	70	55 mg
Scallops	90	33 mg
Shrimp	106	152 mg
Squid (calamari)	92	233 mg

*Per 3½-ounce serving

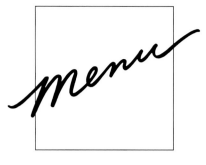

ISLAND BUFFET

Caribbean Jellied Orange Soup

*Mahi-mahi With Lemon
and Pineapple Salsa*

*Steamed and Sautéed Yams,
Carrots, and Long Beans*

*Salad of Artichoke Hearts,
Bibb Lettuce, and Radicchio*

Fresh Tropical Fruit Platter

Nonalcoholic Piña Colada

This light menu suggests the paradise of tropical islands. Prepare the fish ahead, and chill until cooking time. Slice fresh yams and carrots and snip long beans. Sauté lightly in a teaspoon of olive oil, and finish by steaming right before serving. Toss a salad of torn Bibb lettuce, radicchio leaves, and quartered artichoke hearts with a low-calorie vinaigrette dressing. A nonalcoholic Piña Colada (blend pineapple juice and chunks, ice cubes, banana, and coconut flavoring until smooth) is the ideal beverage. A platter of fresh tropical fruits completes the meal. Menu serves four.

CARIBBEAN JELLIED ORANGE SOUP

A refreshing first course, this soup is traditionally served in the Caribbean, where food is designed to cool you. The fresh orange flavor is delicious with seafood or chicken. The consistency of this soup is similar to a consommé, except that it is bright orange in color. The soup should be served chilled in small glass bowls. When entertaining, you can also pass around a bowl of lime slices to those guests who want extra tang.

> 1 quart defatted Chicken Stock (see page 31)
> ½ cup agar flakes or 1 package unflavored gelatin
> 3 cups freshly squeezed orange juice
> 2 egg whites, beaten until frothy
> 1 orange (unpeeled), cut into paper-thin slices
> 12 fresh mint leaves, for garnish (optional)

1. In a large saucepan combine stock with agar flakes and cook 20 minutes over medium heat.

2. Add orange juice to stock and let cool for 15 minutes.

3. Whisk in egg whites. Pour into 4 glass bowls and refrigerate until set (about 45 minutes).

4. Serve chilled, garnished with orange slices and fresh mint leaves, if desired.

Serves 4.

> Calories per serving: 151
> Preparation time: 15 minutes
> Cooking time: 20 minutes
> Chilling time: 1 hour

MAHI-MAHI WITH LEMON AND PINEAPPLE SALSA

A delectable, light-colored fish, mahi-mahi is often served in the Hawaiian Islands, but you can use any firm-fleshed fish, such as salmon or shark, if mahi-mahi is unavailable. The fresh pineapple and lemon salsa is a perfect accompaniment and can be made ahead of time.

For an alternative version of the same recipe, brush on the salsa before grilling. Or you can marinate the fish in the salsa overnight for a stronger citrus flavor.

> ¾ cup fresh pineapple, crushed
> ½ cup minced onion
> ¼ cup minced green bell pepper
> 3 cloves garlic, minced
> ½ cup chopped fresh tomato
> 1 fresh jalapeño chile, seeded and chopped finely
> 1 teaspoon herbal salt substitute
> Juice of 1 lemon
> 4 mahi-mahi steaks
> 2 teaspoons olive oil

1. In a small bowl mix together pineapple, onion, bell pepper, garlic, tomato, jalapeño, salt substitute, and lemon juice. Set salsa aside.

2. Preheat broiler. Lightly brush fish steaks with olive oil. Broil on each side until lightly browned and firm to the touch (about 5 minutes per side). During the last minute of broiling, top with the salsa and finish cooking.

Serves 4.

<u>Note</u> Mahi-mahi should be about 4 to 6 inches from the heat source. If the fish is cooking too fast, lower the broiler rack.

> Calories per serving: 246
> Preparation time: 25 minutes
> Cooking time: 10 minutes

Tropical flavors combine in a refreshing orange soup, broiled mahi-mahi topped with lemon-pineapple salsa, and, for a cool finish, sliced tropical fruits.

Pasta is one of the most versatile foods of low-calorie cuisine. The secret is in the tempting sauces contained in this chapter.

Pasta Perfecta

P asta can be a gourmet, low-calorie addition to any menu if it is made with the right sauces. The calories remain low, and the flavor comes from vegetables, seasonings, and low-fat cheeses instead of cream and butter. A new low-calorie Alfredo sauce is offered in Fettuccine Alfredo With Zucchini and Ricotta (see page 109), and new twists on traditional tomato sauces in two spinach lasagne recipes (see pages 106 and 107). Or you might try the exotic miso pesto in Japanese Pasta (see page 108) or the mustard sauce in Pasta Primavera (also on page 108). Special features explain the differences between fresh and dried pastas (see page 109) and how to make your own fresh pasta at home (see page 110).

Curly spinach spirals are tossed with sweet red pepper strips, whole snow peas, and a light sesame-lemon dressing. Serve Chinese Pasta Salad with steamed Chinese vegetables, such as bok choy or Chinese cabbage, and fruit.

PASTA SALADS

In Italy pasta has long been served at various temperatures, but American epicures have just recently discovered cold pasta salads. What a great way to use up leftover noodles: Simply mix with vegetables, seafood, and a light vinaigrette dressing, and a meal is born. Pasta salads, covered with plastic wrap, usually keep for up to three days.

CHINESE PASTA SALAD

This light and exotic pasta salad is a cinch to make, and it will keep, well covered, for about two days in the refrigerator. If you decide to keep it longer than two to three hours, add the snow peas right before serving, since they tend to discolor quickly.

> 4 cups cooked spiral pasta
> (whole wheat or spinach)
> 1 cup trimmed, whole snow peas
> 2 small red bell peppers, seeded
> and julienned
> 1 teaspoon sesame seed
> ½ teaspoon cayenne pepper, or
> more to taste
> ¼ cup low-sodium tamari or
> soy sauce
> 3 tablespoons dark sesame oil
> 3 tablespoons lemon juice
> 2 tablespoons grated onion
> 2 tablespoons minced garlic
> Dash each dill and freshly
> ground black pepper
> Lettuce leaves, for lining bowl

Combine all ingredients, except lettuce leaves. Let chill for 30 minutes, then serve on lettuce leaves in a bowl.

Serves 4.

> *Calories per serving: 343*
> *Preparation time: 15 minutes*
> *Chilling time: 30 minutes*

FETA SALAD WITH SPIRAL PASTA

This pasta version of traditional Greek salad is made with low-calorie feta cheese, tomatoes, and cucumber, dressed with a light vinaigrette.

> 4 cups cooked spiral pasta
> (white or whole wheat)
> 1 cup crumbled part-skim
> feta cheese
> ¼ cup olive oil
> 1 cup peeled and sliced
> cucumber
> 2 large tomatoes, peeled, seeded,
> and sliced into strips
> ¼ cup pitted Greek olives
> 1 tablespoon dried oregano
> Herbal salt substitute and
> freshly ground pepper, to taste

Combine all ingredients. Let chill for 30 minutes before serving.

Serves 6.

Calories per serving: 305
Preparation time: 20 minutes
Chilling time: 30 minutes

MARINATED MUSHROOM SALAD WITH SHELLS

Here's a simple way to make your own marinated mushrooms and avoid the costly, high-calorie ones sold at the store. In this recipe the mushrooms are tossed with attractively sliced vegetables and a light vermicelli pasta (thin spaghetti). The marinade has a hint of burgundy, which imparts a rich flavor to the salad.

>   2 cups halved button
>   mushrooms
>   ½ cup trimmed snow peas
>   ½ cup seeded and julienned
>   red bell pepper
>   2 tablespoons drained capers
>   1 cup cooked vermicelli pasta,
>   cut into 6-inch lengths
>   2 teaspoons olive oil
>   2 tablespoons red wine vinegar
>   1 tablespoon lemon juice
>   1 tablespoon herbal salt
>   substitute
>   1 tablespoon burgundy wine
>   2 teaspoons honey
>   Dash freshly ground pepper
>   1 teaspoon dill

1. In a large salad bowl, combine mushrooms, snow peas, bell pepper, capers, and pasta. Toss well.

2. In another bowl mix oil, vinegar, lemon juice, salt substitute, burgundy, honey, pepper, and dill. Taste for seasoning. Pour over pasta mixture and mix well.

3. Let chill for 2 hours before serving.

Serves 4.

Calories per serving: 104
Preparation time: 20 minutes
Chilling time: 2 hours

MIDDLE EASTERN PASTA SALAD WITH CHICK-PEAS

This simple salad combines the nutty texture of chick-peas (also known as garbanzo beans and used throughout the Middle East for their exceptional flavor and protein content) with cooked macaroni in a light vinaigrette. Make this salad up to three days in advance—it gets better as it sits.

This salad is an excellent accompaniment to Marinated Beef Kabobs (see page 82) on a dinner menu. For a quick low-calorie lunch, drain some of the vinaigrette and stuff the remaining ingredients with lettuce into pita (pocket) bread.

>   1½ cups cooked chick-peas
>   2 cups cooked macaroni,
>   drained and chilled
>   ¾ cup apple cider vinegar
>   2 tablespoons olive oil
>   1 tablespoon safflower oil
>   ⅓ cup minced parsley
>   ⅓ cup diced red bell pepper
>   ¼ cup minced fresh dill
>   Dash cumin
>   2 tablespoons nutritional yeast
>   Herbal salt substitute and
>   freshly ground pepper, to taste
>   Lettuce, for lining plates or for
>   pocket bread sandwich

Combine all ingredients and chill 2 hours, stirring thoroughly each hour. Serve chilled on a bed of lettuce.

Serves 6.

Calories per serving: 195
Preparation time: 20 minutes
Chilling time: 2 hours

... ON COOKING PASTA

☐ Both fresh and dried pasta require a large amount of boiling water, about 1 quart to every 2 cups of pasta you are cooking. Salting the water helps it boil faster and adds a little flavor to the pasta, but it is not essential if your diet avoids salt. Adding a small amount of oil to the boiling water helps the pasta strands stay separate, but it is unnecessary if you are diligent about stirring the pasta every few minutes.

☐ The trick to successful pasta is the cooking time, which differs considerably between fresh and packaged types. Once the water has boiled, cook dried fettucine and other wide noodles for 7 to 8 minutes, lasagne for 8 to 10 minutes, and fine pasta (such as angel hair) for 5 to 7 minutes, or until al dente. Fresh pasta cooks for only two minutes.

☐ If you're serving immediately, you can drain the freshly cooked pasta and toss it with the sauce or vegetables right away.

☐ If you're not serving for 10 minutes or more, it is advisable to rinse the pasta after cooking. (Pasta continues cooking even after it's out of the pot; unless it's rinsed, it can be surprisingly overcooked by the time you serve it.) Keep the pot of boiling water hot, remove pasta from water using tongs or pasta fork, and refresh it quickly under cold tap water. When it is time to serve, dip the pasta back into the heated water, drain again, and voilà: perfectly cooked pasta every time.

Serve this hearty spinach lasagne with a crisp, green salad and warm French bread for an easy supper. The secret is the rich tomato sauce, flavored with wine and herbs.

LASAGNE AND BAKED PASTA

The following recipes are for hearty eaters, but they are still low calorie. Most fit well into make-ahead menus and are perfect for Sunday night supper with the family.

LOW-CALORIE SPINACH LASAGNE

Because this recipe takes a while to prepare, you may want to make a double batch and freeze half.

   2 *cups each sliced onions and sliced mushrooms*
   1 *cup white wine*
   2 *cups chopped spinach leaves*
   1 *tablespoon herbal salt substitute*
   1 *cup crumbled firm tofu*
   1 *cup farmer cheese or part-skim ricotta cheese*
     Oil, for greasing baking dish
   1 *package (16 oz) spinach lasagne noodles, cooked and drained*
   2 *tablespoons Parmesan cheese mixed with ¼ cup bread crumbs*

Lasagne Tomato Sauce

   ½ *cup white wine*
   1 *small onion, chopped finely*
   ½ *cup sliced mushrooms*
   2 *cloves garlic, minced*
   ½ *cup chopped carrots*
   ½ *cup chopped celery*
   ⅛ *teaspoon ground nutmeg*
   3 *cups plum tomatoes (canned or fresh), chopped*
   1 *teaspoon dried basil*
   ½ *teaspoon dried oregano*

1. Prepare Lasagne Tomato Sauce. While sauce is cooking, sauté onions and mushrooms in white wine over medium heat until soft (about 10 minutes). Add spinach leaves and salt substitute and cook, covered, for 1 minute.

2. Remove from heat and mix with tofu and farmer cheese. Set aside.

3. Preheat oven to 375° F. Lightly oil a 9- by 12-inch baking dish.

4. Assemble lasagne by layering spinach filling, sauce, and noodles. Repeat twice, using all ingredients and ending with noodles on top.

5. Sprinkle lasagne with the Parmesan–bread crumb mixture. Bake lasagne for 30 minutes.

Serves 6 to 8.

Lasagne Tomato Sauce

1. In a medium saucepan heat wine; add onion, mushrooms, garlic, carrots, and celery. Sauté over medium-high heat for 15 minutes. Add nutmeg, tomatoes, basil, and oregano. Cover and cook over medium heat for 30 minutes, stirring frequently.

2. Purée sauce in blender. Set aside.

Calories per serving: 365
Preparation time: 45 minutes
Cooking time: 55 minutes
Baking time: 30 minutes

RAISIN AND APPLE KUGEL

Kugel is a dish of German and Austrian origin, a sweet noodle and cheese mixture that is baked to a crisp crust. This fruit-flavored version has apples and raisins studding the layers of noodles and cheese. It can be made up to three days ahead, and keeps, covered, in the refrigerator, but does not freeze well.

> Oil, for baking dish
> 2 teaspoons melted butter
> 2 tablespoons honey
> 2 tablespoons Neufchâtel cheese
> 1 cup part-skim cottage cheese
> 1 cup nonfat, plain yogurt
> 2 tablespoons cinnamon
> 1 teaspoon herbal salt substitute
> 2 egg whites, beaten
> 2 whole eggs, beaten
> ½ cup raisins
> 3 sweet apples, such as red or golden Delicious, cored and sliced thin
> ½ package (8 oz) egg or whole wheat lasagne noodles, cooked and drained
> ⅓ cup nonfat milk

1. Preheat oven to 400° F. Lightly oil a 9- by 12-inch baking dish.

2. In a mixing bowl combine butter, honey, Neufchâtel, cottage cheese, yogurt, cinnamon, salt substitute, egg whites, and whole eggs. In another bowl combine raisins and apples.

3. Layer kugel by alternating cheese mixture, noodles, and fruit mixture, ending with noodles. Pour milk over the top.

4. Bake for 40 minutes, then let cool and slice into squares.

Serves 8.

> *Calories per serving: 220*
> *Preparation time: 20 minutes*
> *Baking time: 40 minutes*

GREEN AND WHITE LASAGNE

The name of this lasagne derives from the alternating layers of spinach and white cheeses. An herbed tomato sauce is added before baking, but the lasagne can be assembled without the sauce, covered, and refrigerated for up to 48 hours, and then topped with the sauce before baking. It also freezes well.

> 1 teaspoon safflower oil, plus oil for greasing dish
> 1 cup each chopped onions and chopped mushrooms
> 2 tablespoons minced almonds
> 4 cups (packed) spinach leaves
> 2 cups part-skim ricotta cheese
> 4 green onions, minced
> ¼ cup minced parsley
> 3 tablespoons minced fresh basil
> 2 tablespoons grated Parmesan cheese
> 1 package (16 oz) spinach lasagne noodles, cooked and drained

Herb-Tomato Sauce

> 1 teaspoon olive oil
> ⅓ cup white wine
> 3 tablespoons chopped fresh basil
> ½ teaspoon dried thyme
> ¼ teaspoon dried oregano
> 2 tablespoons whole wheat pastry flour
> 2 cups nonfat milk
> 1 cup chopped fresh tomatoes
> ⅛ teaspoon nutmeg

1. Prepare Herb-Tomato Sauce. In clean skillet heat safflower oil and sauté onions until soft but not browned. Add mushrooms and almonds and continue to cook until mushrooms weep moisture. Add spinach leaves, cover, and steam (using moisture in pan) over medium heat for 3 minutes. Remove from heat and set aside.

2. Preheat oven to 375° F. Mix together ricotta, green onions, parsley, basil, and Parmesan. Set aside. Lightly oil a 9- by 12-inch baking dish.

3. Purée the sauce in a blender. Assemble lasagne by alternating layers of spinach sauté, noodles, and cheese mixture, ending up with noodles on top. Pour the sauce over all. Bake lasagne until bubbly and lightly browned (about 45 minutes).

Serves 8.

Herb-Tomato Sauce

1. In a medium skillet heat olive oil and white wine; add basil, thyme, and oregano and cook for 1 minute at medium heat. Stir in flour and cook 2 minutes over low heat, stirring frequently. Slowly add milk and cook sauce to the thickness of heavy cream.

2. Add tomatoes and nutmeg. Cover and continue to cook over low heat for 20 minutes, while preparing lasagne filling.

> *Calories per serving: 388*
> *Preparation time: 40 minutes*
> *Baking time: 45 minutes*

LIGHT PASTA DISHES

From a simple fettuccine Alfredo, to a rich basil tomato sauce, to an exotic chilled *pasta primavera*, the following dishes are easy to prepare and are winners with family and guests.

PASTA PRIMAVERA WITH MUSTARD SAUCE

This springtime pasta recipe is best made with a sweet mustard rather than a wine-flavored Dijon. Make this recipe right before serving for best flavor; it doesn't freeze well.

- ½ cup chopped, peeled prawns
- 2 teaspoons olive oil
- 1 large onion, chopped
- 4 cloves garlic, minced
- 1 red bell pepper, seeded and coarsely chopped
- 1 small zucchini, sliced into thin rounds
- 1 cup fresh peas
- 1 teaspoon chopped fresh basil
- 1 teaspoon chopped chives
- 1 cup plain, nonfat yogurt
- 1 teaspoon honey
- ⅓ cup sweet mustard
- 1 pound bow-tie pasta
  Freshly ground black pepper, to taste

1. In a large skillet sauté prawns in olive oil until they turn bright pink (about 1 minute). Remove from skillet and set aside.

2. In the same pan sauté onion until soft, adding a little water if the pan gets too dry. Add garlic, bell pepper, and zucchini. Cook for 5 more minutes.

3. Add peas, basil, and chives. Cook until peas turn bright green. Remove from heat and mix with prawns. Stir in yogurt, honey, and mustard and mix well.

4. Cook pasta in boiling water until tender (about 8 minutes). Drain and toss with sauce. Season with black pepper.

Serves 6.

Calories per serving: 190
Preparation time: 25 minutes
Cooking time: 8–10 minutes

EGGPLANT AND YELLOW PEPPER VERMICELLI

If you can't find yellow bell peppers, make this recipe with green or red bell peppers (although the color combination won't be as striking). The Mediterranean flavor of this dish comes from the fresh basil, a taste of olive oil, Greek olives, and capers. The sautéed vegetables can be cooked up to four hours ahead of time and combined with the pasta just before serving.

- ¼ cup olive oil
- ¼ to ½ cup white wine
- 2 cloves garlic, minced
- 2 cups chopped tomato
- 2 small Japanese-style eggplants, peeled and cubed
- 2 sweet yellow bell peppers
- 2 tablespoons pitted Greek olives
- 2 tablespoons capers
- 2 tablespoons chopped fresh basil
- 6 cups cooked spaghetti or fettuccine
- 3 tablespoons grated Parmesan cheese
  Freshly ground black pepper, to taste

1. In a skillet heat olive oil and ¼ cup wine and sauté garlic for 1 minute at medium-high heat. Add tomato and eggplants and continue to cook, stirring frequently, for 10 minutes more. If the mixture dries out too fast, lower the heat, and add ¼ cup more wine.

2. Preheat broiler. Cut bell peppers in half and seed them. Place cut side down on an aluminum-foil-lined baking sheet and broil until skins turn black (about 5 minutes). Place blackened peppers into a paper bag and seal top. Let peppers sweat in the bag for 10 minutes, then remove and rinse under cold water, rubbing off the blackened skin with your fingers. Chop the peeled peppers coarsely and add to the sauté.

3. Add olives, capers, and basil to sauté. Reheat spaghetti in heated water for 1 minute, then drain and toss with sauté. Season with Parmesan and black pepper and serve immediately.

Serves 6.

Calories per serving: 329
Preparation time: 25 minutes

JAPANESE PASTA WITH MISO PESTO

Pesto is a puréed or mashed mixture of fresh herbs, nuts, oil, garlic, and cheeses. Here is a slightly different version, low on calories and strong on flavor. This recipe substitutes a Japanese miso paste, similar in taste to very mild soy sauce, for the cheese, making the pesto free of dairy products. The miso is tossed with cooked Japanese *soba* noodles, made from buckwheat. Both soba and miso can be found in Asian markets or health-food stores.

- 3 cups loosely packed fresh basil leaves
- 2 packages (16 oz each) soba noodles
- 1 tablespoon olive oil
- 2 cloves minced garlic
- 2 tablespoons miso paste, preferably light colored
- 1 tablespoon walnuts or almonds

1. Chop basil very finely. Cook and drain soba noodles. Toss basil with hot soba.

2. In a blender purée together olive oil, garlic, miso, and walnuts. Toss with pasta and basil and serve hot.

Serves 4 to 6.

Calories per serving: 443
Preparation time: 15 minutes
Cooking time: 8–10 minutes

MARY'S CHUNKY TOMATO SAUCE WITH FRESH BASIL

This sauce tastes as if it's been cooking for hours when actually it's been on the stove for only 30 minutes. The secret is in the presoaking of the dried herbs. Like perfume manufacturers distilling the essential oils of flowers and herbs by steeping them in alcohol, the herbs in this recipe are steeped in room-temperature wine in order to release the flavors without lengthy cooking time. This sauce can easily be doubled or tripled, freezes well, and makes a great gift.

- 2 tablespoons chopped fresh basil
- 1 tablespoon dried oregano
- ½ cup dry sherry
- 1 teaspoon olive oil
- ½ cup white wine
- 1 small onion, finely chopped
- 2 large red bell peppers, seeded and chopped
- 2 cups chopped mushrooms
- 4 large, very ripe tomatoes, coarsely chopped
- 3 large cloves garlic, minced
- ¼ cup tomato paste

1. In a small bowl place basil, oregano, and sherry and let steep for 15 minutes at room temperature.

2. In a medium saucepan over medium-high heat, combine olive oil and white wine. Add onion and cook slowly until soft but not browned. Add bell peppers and cook for 5 minutes.

3. Add mushrooms and continue cooking, stirring frequently, until they weep moisture. Add tomatoes, garlic, and tomato paste; cook for 10 minutes more.

4. Pour sherry and herb mixture into sauce and bring to a boil. Lower heat to medium-high and simmer sauce for 10 minutes. Serve hot over pasta.

Makes approximately 3 cups.

Calories per ½ cup serving: 97
Preparation time: 20 minutes
Cooking time: 30 minutes

FETTUCCINE ALFREDO WITH ZUCCHINI AND RICOTTA

Alfredo sauces often contain up to one cup of cream per serving. They usually also contain an equal amount of grated Parmesan. This one, however, makes use of part-skim ricotta and adds grated, sautéed vegetables for more flavor and fewer calories. This Fettuccine Alfredo variation keeps well and can be reheated, but do not freeze this dish.

- 2 teaspoons olive oil
- ¼ cup dry sherry
- 1 cup sliced onion
- 1½ packed cups grated zucchini
- 4 cloves garlic, minced
- ½ cup nonfat milk
- 2 tablespoons grated Parmesan cheese
- 1½ cups part-skim ricotta cheese
- 4 cups cooked fettuccine

1. In a skillet heat oil and sherry and sauté onion until soft but not browned. Add zucchini and garlic and cook for 5 minutes.

2. Combine milk and cheeses. Add to sauté and cook at medium heat until thick (about 10 minutes). Toss with cooked pasta and serve hot.

Serves 6.

Note Ricotta, a cow's milk cheese made from whey, is mild, creamy, and moist, and should be used when very fresh. Traditionally, it is an important ingredient in many Italian dishes, from lasagne and cannelloni to cheesecake.

Calories per serving: 282
Preparation time: 15 minutes
Cooking time: 8–10 minutes

FRESH AND DRIED PASTAS

There's a noticeable difference between fresh and dried pasta. Fresh pasta has a melt-in-your-mouth texture and flavor, and is sought after by gourmet cooks. Supermarkets offer a wide variety of packaged fresh pastas in the delicatessen sections—from bright green spinach fettuccine to pale artichoke spaghetti. Flavored pastas are made by adding a small amount of dried or powdered vegetables to the dough while the dough is being mixed.

Try combining different types of pasta in one dish. For example, a quick sauté of bright vegetables—such as red and green bell peppers, yellow summer squash, white onion, and fresh shiitake mushrooms—can be paired with cooked artichoke and spinach noodles and garnished with chopped cilantro and parsley for a quick yet vivid dish.

You can experiment with different shapes and sizes of pasta, which are usually available in gourmet shops. For example, stuff manicotti (thick, hollow tube noodles) with any of the lasagne fillings found on pages 106 and 107. Or try large pasta shells packed with minced sautéed vegetables and covered with Mary's Chunky Tomato Sauce With Fresh Basil. Both recipes can be baked at 350° F for 25 minutes. These dried hollow pasta shapes can be used right out of the package if you are baking them later with a sauce (as for the above stuffed shells); they will soften in the oven. Otherwise, cook dried pasta until al dente (8 to 10 minutes) or until soft but still holding a shape.

HOW TO MAKE YOUR OWN PASTA

Making your own fresh pasta is easier than you think. With only a bowl, a fork, and a rolling pin, you can turn out professional-quality pasta in 10 minutes, dry it for 15 to 20 minutes, and then serve it up in 5 more. The secret to successful homemade pasta is to keep from overworking the dough—it must stay soft and pliable, but not sticky.

The following ingredients may be used for a basic whole wheat or white egg noodle pasta, but you can create a variety of other flavored pastas—zucchini, broccoli, onion, and so on—by combining these ingredients with the flour.

> 1 cup whole wheat pastry or white pastry flour, plus flour for kneading
> 1 egg
> 1 teaspoon olive oil (optional)
> Pinch herbal salt substitute
> ½ cup (approximately) water, or as needed

1. In a bowl mix flour and salt together, with a fork. Make a well in the center of the flour and add egg, and oil, if desired. (Olive oil will help make the dough smooth but is not essential in this low-calorie recipe.)

2. Slowly incorporate flour into the well, mixing with egg, until a stiff dough is formed. If mixture seems dry, dribble in a little water. (If you are using a food processor to mix ingredients, insert ingredients, set to "pulse" speed, and process for about 1 minute or until mixture begins to pull away from the sides of the container.)

3. Lightly flour your hands and a kneading surface, such as a bread board or countertop. Knead rapidly for 5 minutes. Dough should be soft, pliable, and unsticky. When dough is in the form of a ball, make sure it is not sticky. Add more flour or water as needed, but add flour gradually, as too much flour makes a tough dough. At this point, you can test dough by stretching it a few inches in your hands; it should not break.

4. Place ball of dough on a lightly floured surface and flatten it slightly by hand. Roll out dough with a lightly floured rolling pin (or any clean, smooth, cylindrical object). Roll dough from the center to the outer edges, flipping the dough frequently, until it is in the form of a flat rectangle, about 1/16 inch thick (about the thickness of a quarter).

5. Flour both sides of dough well and roll into a cylindrical (jelly roll) shape. Cut the roll into desired width (usually ¼ inch). Unwind each strip and shake off excess flour.

6. Let the strips dry on a dry cloth towel on counter or hang to air dry on pasta rack. Pasta should dry 15 to 30 minutes before cooking or 3 hours before storing. Pasta can be stored in the freezer while still fresh or on the shelf if it is well dried.

Serves 2.

PASTA MACHINES

If you happen to own a pasta machine—either the electric or hand-crank type—pasta making can really be a breeze! If using a machine, make sure the dough is floured very well before rolling or cutting because the machine will tend to make the strips of dough stick together more than when cutting by hand.

Most pasta machines have at least two cutting attachments: one for wide noodles and one for thin spaghetti. Use the wide-noodle attachment for recipes that call for creamy sauces as the sauce will stick better to wider pasta.

Before cleaning pasta machines, read the instructions. Water can cause rusting or sticking, and you may be better off removing excess dough and flour with a small brush.

TREVOR'S SPAGHETTI NEAPOLITAN

Created in Brisbane, Australia, this tasty mixture of cooked spaghetti and sautéed vegetables in a light cream sauce is served cold. It will keep two or three days, tightly covered, in the refrigerator and is excellent for a chilled summer lunch.

> 4 cups cooked spaghetti, chopped into 4- to 6-inch lengths
> 1 teaspoon each safflower oil, olive oil, and butter
> 1 cup sliced onion
> ½ cup each chopped green bell pepper and red bell pepper
> ½ cup each sliced mushrooms and sliced zucchini
> 2 tablespoons whole wheat pastry flour
> 1 cup nonfat milk
> ⅓ cup fresh peas
> Herbal salt substitute and freshly ground pepper, to taste

1. Place cooked pasta in a large bowl and begin chilling while you prepare vegetables.

2. In a skillet heat oils and butter and sauté onion over medium heat for 3 minutes, stirring frequently, without browning it. Add bell peppers, mushrooms, and zucchini, and cook until mushrooms weep moisture (4 to 5 more minutes). Add flour and cook, stirring, over low heat for 2 minutes.

3. Pour in milk and heat through. Add peas, salt substitute, and pepper and toss with chilled pasta. Continue to chill the dish for up to 2 hours.

Serves 6.

> *Calories per serving: 181*
> *Preparation time: 20 minutes*
> *Chilling time: 2 hours*

PASTA SHELLS WITH PEAS AND PROSCIUTTO

A small taste of calorie-rich prosciutto ham is added to this recipe for flavor and color. Make the dish just before serving in order to keep the peas bright.

- 1 teaspoon olive oil
- ¼ cup dry sherry
- ½ cup sliced red bell pepper
- 1 tablespoon minced garlic
- ⅓ cup cooked prosciutto ham, fat trimmed off
- ¼ cup fresh basil, chopped
- 2 tablespoons parsley, chopped
- 1 teaspoon dried thyme
- 1 cup fresh peas
- 4 cups cooked small pasta shells
- 2 tablespoons Parmesan cheese

In a skillet heat oil and sherry and sauté bell pepper and garlic for 3 minutes. Add ham, basil, parsley, thyme, peas, pasta, and Parmesan and cook until peas turn bright green (about one minute). Serve hot.

Serves 4.

Calories per serving: 289
Preparation time: 20 minutes

PASTA WITH MARINATED ARTICHOKE HEARTS

You can buy artichokes premarinated, or toss drained, canned artichoke hearts in a light lemon-juice vinaigrette for the same effect. Combine the pasta and sauce right before serving.

- 2 teaspoons olive oil
- 2 tablespoons minced garlic
- 1 cup cooked, shredded chicken
- ¼ cup white wine
- ½ cup sliced mushrooms
- ¼ cup minced red bell pepper
- 3 tablespoons minced parsley
- ½ cup nonfat, plain yogurt
- 1 teaspoon honey
- 4 cups cooked spiral pasta
- 6 ounces marinated, drained artichoke hearts

1. In a skillet heat oil and sauté garlic and chicken for 2 minutes, stirring frequently. Remove garlic and chicken to a bowl; set aside.

2. In same skillet heat wine and sauté mushroom and bell pepper until mushrooms weep moisture. Remove from heat and combine with chicken and garlic in bowl.

3. Add parsley, yogurt, honey, pasta, and artichoke hearts; toss well. Serve at once.

Serves 4.

Calories per serving: 333
Preparation time: 20 minutes

An out-of-this-world recipe, Pasta Shells With Peas and Prosciutto will become a favorite for entertaining. The sauce is made with sherry, olive oil, and fresh basil and complements the sharp, salty flavor of the ham.

Choose the natural sweetness of fresh fruit to create memorable desserts that satisfy the sweet tooth without expanding the waistline.

Not-So-Sinful Desserts

E ven the dieter needs to satisfy a sweet
tooth occasionally. But instead of
a high-calorie binge, try these satisfying
yet low-calorie desserts made with fresh fruit,
yogurt, low-fat milk, and small amounts of
wines and liqueurs. Fruit desserts include
Jamaican Fried Bananas With Rum (see page
117) and Wine-Basted Pears (see page 115).
Mousse-lovers should try Peach Mousse
(see page 118) or Tofu-Strawberry Mousse
(see page 119). And pastry lovers should not
miss Lemon Dream Cheesecake (see page 122)
or Sweet Potato Cream Pie (see page 123).
Easy-to-follow instructions will guide you in
making low-calorie iced desserts (see page
119) and handling the fragile filo dough (see
page 123) for two tasty tart recipes.

The natural sweetness of fresh pears complements the tangy orange-wine sauce. Garnish elegant Wine-Basted Pears with mint and strips of orange peel.

FRUIT DESSERTS

Fresh fruit offers natural sweetness to low-calorie desserts, if prepared correctly. Or, you can supplement the natural fruit sugars with unprocessed, unrefined sweeteners such as maple syrup, undiluted apple juice concentrate, and honey.

BAKED PEARS

Baked Pears works as a brunch dessert, an early morning breakfast starter, or a final course to a light summer lunch of seafood salad. Either make Baked Pears ahead of time and chill them slightly during warm weather or serve them hot from the oven in cooler weather.

>   6 large pears, slightly underripe
>   ¼ cup lemon juice
>   1 cup orange juice
>   2 tablespoons maple syrup
>   ¼ teaspoon allspice

1. Preheat oven to 350° F. With a melon baller, core pears by pressing the melon baller into the bottom of the pear. Then insert the melon baller into the cavity and scoop out any

remaining core. Peel pears, but leave them whole.

2. Mix remaining ingredients for poaching liquid. Place pears in a deep baking dish and pour liquid over them. Bake until pears are softened (about 45 minutes). Serve with a small amount of poaching liquid. Pears can be served either hot or chilled.

Serves 6.

> *Calories per serving: 123*
> *Preparation time: 20 minutes*
> *Baking time: 45 minutes*

APPLES STUFFED WITH RAISINS AND DATES

A simple dish that brings back memories of mom's cooking, this very low-calorie dessert is perfect for fall, when tart apples are in season. The stuffed apples are also nice for a brunch starter. They will keep well, tightly covered, for up to six days in the refrigerator.

>   6 large tart baking apples, such as Granny Smith or McIntosh
>   2 dried figs, chopped
>   ¼ cup pitted, chopped fresh dates
>   ¼ cup raisins, soaked in hot water for 10 minutes, then drained
>   1 teaspoon cinnamon
>   1 teaspoon nutmeg
>   4 tablespoons frozen apple juice concentrate

1. Preheat oven to 350° F. Core apples with apple corer or sharp knife, leaving a small bit of fruit at the bottom to hold the filling.

2. Mix remaining ingredients and stuff into apples, packing well.

3. Place fruit in a shallow baking dish and cover loosely with aluminum foil. Fill with water to ¼ height of apples. Bake until apples are soft and browned (about 35 minutes). Serve hot or cold.

Serves 6.

> *Calories per serving: 201*
> *Preparation time: 15 minutes*
> *Baking time: 35 minutes*

WINE-BASTED PEARS

Many people think that wine is incompatible with light cuisine, but it isn't—as long as the wine is heated to the boiling point. The alcohol in wine (the source of most of its calories) evaporates when you heat a wine mixture to 170° F. The aroma and flavor remain—but about 80 percent of the wine's original calories evaporate.

When you serve a pasta or chicken entrée, this wine-basted fruit dish is a delightful finish to the meal, especially if you use the same red wine to poach the pears as you serve with the main course. Make these up to one week ahead of time and serve chilled. Save the poaching liquid. It will keep for four months in the refrigerator and can be used again to poach more fruit.

- 6 *large pears, slightly underripe*
- 2 *tablespoons lemon juice*
- 2 *cups hearty red wine, such as Zinfandel or burgundy*
- 1 *teaspoon honey*
- 2 *teaspoons cinnamon*
- 1 *cup orange juice*
  Fresh mint leaves, for garnish

1. Core whole pears from bottom, using a melon baller, leaving stems intact. Peel the pears.

2. In a deep saucepan mix remaining ingredients except garnish and bring to a boil. Add pears and simmer until they become deep red in color and softened (about 35 minutes). Drain pears and chill, reserving liquid for another use. Garnish pears with mint leaves and serve.

Serves 6.

Calories per serving: 200
Preparation time: 20 minutes
Cooking time: 35 minutes
Chilling time: 1 hour

FRUIT COMPOTE WITH YOGURT SAUCE

A compote is a stewed mixture of dried fruits, such as prunes, apricots, and figs. After it cooks, it can be puréed for a topping, or served with another topping, such as the sweetened yogurt sauce (plain, nonfat yogurt with a dash of maple syrup) used here. It is a very easy, make-ahead dessert. For a smart presentation, serve fruit compote in large wineglasses and garnish with fresh mint or grated orange peel.

- 1 *cup chopped, pitted dried dates*
- 2 *cups chopped, pitted dried prunes*
- 1 *cup chopped dried apricots*
- ½ *cup raisins*
- 1 *cup chopped dried figs*
- 1 *cup cored and grated apple*
- 1 *teaspoon ground cardamom*
- 1 *teaspoon cinnamon*
- 1 *teaspoon grated orange rind*
- 3 *cups apple juice*
- 2 *tablespoons lemon juice*
- ½ *cup plain, nonfat yogurt*
- ½ *teaspoon maple syrup*
- ⅛ *teaspoon nutmeg*
- ¼ *cup puréed fresh or frozen strawberries (optional)*

1. Place dates, prunes, apricots, raisins, figs, apple, cardamom, cinnamon, orange rind, and apple and lemon juices into a heavy saucepan and bring to a boil.

2. Lower heat, cover, and simmer for 45 minutes, stirring occasionally.

3. While mixture is cooking, in a small bowl combine yogurt, maple syrup, nutmeg, and puréed strawberries, if desired; mix well. Chill and serve over cooked compote.

Serves 8.

Calories per serving: 379
Preparation time: 10 minutes
Cooking time: 45 minutes–1 hour

SUMMER MELON BOUQUETS WITH MINT SAUCE

An easy way to make the most of fresh summer fruit, this eye-catching dessert is served in a scooped-out melon shell. Make this recipe as close to serving time as possible to retain the color and texture of the fresh fruit. You can use an assortment of fresh fruit in season, but cantaloupe and watermelon offer a nice blend of color.

- 1 *small watermelon, cut in half lengthwise*
- 1 *cup cantaloupe balls*
- 1 *cup (8 oz can) lichee nuts, rinsed and drained*
- 1 *cup pineapple chunks*
- 1 *cup (8 oz can) mandarin orange slices, rinsed and drained*
- 1 *cup halved strawberries*
- ¼ *cup maple syrup*
- ¼ *cup date sugar (ground, dried dates) or honey*
- 3 *tablespoons chopped fresh mint, plus mint leaves for garnish*

1. Scoop the flesh out of the watermelon shells. Using a melon baller, make 2 cups of watermelon balls from the flesh and reserve the remainder for another use.

2. Mix watermelon balls with remaining ingredients, except garnish. Spoon into one of the watermelon shells. Chill for 15 minutes.

3. Garnish with mint leaves and serve out of the shell.

Serves 8.

Calories per serving: 308
Preparation time: 25 minutes
Chilling time: 15 minutes

... ON SWEETENING WITHOUT GRANULATED SUGARS

For low-calorie sweetening rely on the natural sugar in fresh and dried fruits or on the less-refined sweeteners that are available on the market. Besides being healthier, the natural sugar contained in honey, fruits, and vegetables has almost twice the sweetness of granulated table sugar. Therefore, you do not need to use as much natural sugar in recipes and will thus, in most cases, save calories. Here are some tips about substituting natural ingredients in recipes that call for granulated or brown sugar.

☐ Apple juice concentrate. Frozen, undiluted apple juice works well in puddings, custards, cakes, pies, and sweet breads.

☐ Date sugar. Ground, dried dates can replace brown or granulated sugar in most recipes.

☐ Maple syrup. A small amount will sweeten a lot, and is good in custards, fruit desserts, sauces, and pies.

☐ Honey. A light, clear honey can be used in most recipes that call for white sugar.

☐ Puréed raisins or dates. Used in fruit desserts, cobblers, and pies, puréed raisins or dates are also good with dark cakes, such as fruitcake or spice cake.

The general rule of thumb for substituting liquid sweeteners for dry ones is as follows: For every 1 cup of sugar that is omitted use ¾ cup liquid sweetener (or less to taste); add 2 tablespoons more of flour and subtract 2 tablespoons of oil or butter.

RHUBARB AND STRAWBERRY COBBLER WITH GRANOLA CRUST

This delicious cobbler is a fine dessert in the spring and summer when strawberries and rhubarb are at their peaks. You may also use frozen fruit with almost equally good results. The filling may also be used for a pie filling; it is bright and colorful, and tangy with the sweet-sour flavor of the rhubarb.

    3 cups chopped rhubarb
    2 cups sliced strawberries
    ½ cup maple syrup
    2 tablespoons arrowroot powder
    1 egg
    1 teaspoon cinnamon
    ¼ cup puréed, pitted fresh dates
    1 teaspoon cornmeal
    2 cups rolled oats
    ½ teaspoon vanilla
    2 tablespoons frozen apple juice
       concentrate
    ¼ teaspoon allspice
    ¼ teaspoon mace
       Safflower oil, for greasing
       baking sheet

1. Preheat oven to 400° F. Place rhubarb and strawberries in a deep baking dish.

2. In a blender purée maple syrup, arrowroot, egg, cinnamon, and dates. Pour over rhubarb mixture. Cover loosely with aluminum foil and bake for 30 minutes.

3. While fruit is baking, in a bowl combine the remaining ingredients except oil. Mix well. Place on a lightly oiled baking sheet and bake for 20 minutes, in the same 400° F oven, stirring every 5 minutes to evenly brown.

4. During last 5 minutes of baking remove both dishes from oven. Remove aluminum-foil cover from rhubarb mixture; sprinkle mixture with the granola and return to oven. Bake for 5 minutes. Serve warm or cold.

Serves 6 to 8.

Calories per serving: 191
Preparation time: 20 minutes
Baking time: 50 minutes

APPLE-CRANBERRY COBBLER

Apples, tangy cranberries, and pears under a granola-type crust can be served in small glass bowls for an inviting conclusion to a holiday meal. Pass a bowl of nonfat yogurt as a topping. You can make Apple-Cranberry Cobbler ahead of time and keep it, covered, in the refrigerator for up to five days.

    3   cups sliced apple
    1   cup fresh or frozen
        cranberries
    1   cup sliced pear
    2   teaspoons cinnamon
    ¼   cup chopped pitted fresh dates
    1   tablespoon arrowroot powder
    ¼   teaspoon lemon juice
    ¼   cup maple syrup
    1½ cups rolled oats
    ¼   teaspoon vanilla
    ¾   cup apple juice
    1   teaspoon nutmeg

1. Preheat oven to 375° F. In a shallow baking dish, combine apples, cranberries, and pears.

2. In a blender purée cinnamon, dates, arrowroot, lemon juice, and maple syrup, and pour over apple mixture.

3. Combine oats, vanilla, apple juice, and nutmeg and mix with your fingers or a wooden spoon until the apple juice is distributed evenly. Sprinkle topping over apples.

4. Bake until bubbly and slightly browned (about 40 minutes).

Serves 6 to 8.

Calories per serving: 160
Preparation time: 20 minutes
Baking time: 40 minutes

JAMAICAN FRIED BANANAS WITH RUM

Although usually a very high-calorie dessert, these fried bananas are cooked in a light syrup of date sugar and small amounts of butter and white rum. It is important to cook the rum long enough to burn off the alcohol, thus reducing the calories considerably. Make this dessert close to serving time, so the bananas retain their shape.

 6 *large bananas in the peel*
 1 *teaspoon butter*
 ½ *cup apple juice*
 ½ *cup white rum*
 ¼ *cup date sugar (ground, dried dates)*
 ½ *teaspoon nutmeg*

1. Preheat the oven to 400° F. Place unpeeled bananas on a baking sheet. Prick the skin of each banana several times with the prongs of a fork. Cook bananas until they turn black (about 10 minutes).

2. In a large skillet combine remaining ingredients and cook over medium-high heat for 8 minutes (to burn off alcohol).

3. Carefully peel one side of each banana and place it, open side down, in the rum syrup. Remove the remaining peel. Cut each banana in half and cook, turning once, until lightly golden (about 2 minutes). Serve warm.

Serves 6.

Calories per serving: 183
Preparation time: 5 minutes
Cooking time: 20 minutes

Ripe bananas are baked in their skins, then peeled and sautéed in a light syrup of date sugar, apple juice, and white rum. Serve Jamaican Fried Bananas as part of a stir-fry menu.

PUDDINGS AND MOUSSES

Treat yourself to an old-fashioned rice pudding, a sweet strawberry or peach mousse, or a lemon iced dessert, and you needn't worry about your diet. The following recipes use low-fat dairy products, such as nonfat milk and plain yogurt, to cut calories dramatically on these otherwise-rich desserts. The creamy texture and refreshing flavor of yogurt makes it a perfect ingredient for mousses and puddings. In addition, a tablespoon of plain low-fat yogurt contains only about 10 calories.

PEACH MOUSSE

A very light concoction of fresh fruit, yogurt, and spices, this cooked mousse is chilled in a decorative mold or in wineglasses for an exquisite presentation.

- 3 cups sliced peaches
- 3 eggs
- ¼ cup yogurt
- 2 tablespoons arrowroot powder
- 1 teaspoon maple syrup
  Sliced fresh peaches, for garnish

1. In a blender combine all ingredients except for garnish and purée until smooth.

2. Pour into a saucepan and stir over low heat, until thickened to the consistency of custard.

3. Spoon into a decorative mold or 4 wineglasses. Chill for 1 hour. Garnish with sliced fresh peaches.

Serves 4.

> *Calories per serving: 141*
> *Preparation time: 20 minutes*
> *Chilling time: 1 hour*

NAN'S LEMON SNOW

This recipe, adapted from a new cookbook by restaurateur Nan Narboe of Portland, Oregon, is a pleasant froth of a dessert, fun to eat because it dissolves in your mouth like meringue cookies do. Serve it swirled into wineglasses, garnished with grated lemon peel, or pair it with a sauce of fresh berries. You can prepare this recipe the evening before but no earlier, as it will lose its texture.

- 1 envelope unflavored gelatin
- ½ cup frozen apple juice concentrate, thawed
- ⅔ cup boiling water
- ⅓ cup fresh lemon juice
- ½ teaspoon grated lemon rind (optional)
- 3 egg whites

1. Sprinkle gelatin over apple juice concentrate in a mixing bowl.

2. Pour boiling water over softened gelatin and stir to dissolve.

3. Add lemon juice and taste. For more lemony flavor, add more juice and lemon rind.

4. Chill mixture about 30 minutes in fridge or 15 minutes in freezer, stirring occasionally.

5. Add egg whites and whip mixture with a balloon whisk or an electric handheld beater until it triples in volume and resembles a soft meringue.

6. Spoon into wineglasses and chill at least 4 hours or overnight. To serve with berries, form "meringue baskets" on dessert plates with large spoon. Chill, then fill with berries just before serving.

Serves 8 to 10.

> *Calories per serving: 54*
> *Preparation time: 20 minutes*
> *Chilling time: 4 hours or overnight*

ORANGE RICE PUDDING

This rich pudding was altered to cut the number of calories. Rice pudding is an old favorite of many, and this one adds a hint of citrus to the standard recipe. It can be made ahead, freezes well, and can be served either warm or cold.

- 4 cups nonfat milk
- 2 tablespoons maple syrup
  Pinch herbal salt substitute
- 1 cup uncooked long-grain brown rice
- 1½ teaspoons vanilla
- 1 cup raisins
- ⅓ cup chopped, pitted fresh dates
- 1 tablespoon grated orange rind
- ½ cup orange juice
  Safflower oil, for greasing baking dish
  Orange peel strips, for garnish

1. In a heavy 2-quart saucepan, combine 2 cups of the milk, the maple syrup, salt substitute, and rice. Bring to a boil and lower heat to simmer. Cook 25 minutes over medium heat.

2. Preheat oven to 325° F. Mix together the remaining ingredients except oil. Lightly oil a 9- by 12-inch baking dish.

3. Mix rice mixture with orange juice mixture and pour into the prepared baking dish. Bake until solidified and lightly browned (about 90 minutes). Garnish with strips of orange peel.

Serves 8.

> *Calories per serving: 228*
> *Preparation time: 10 minutes*
> *Cooking time: 25 minutes*
> *Baking time: 90 minutes*

STEAMED PUMPKIN PUDDING

This dessert is perfect for fall days, when pumpkins are plentiful and a warm dish is welcome. The pudding is baked in a bundt or cake pan placed inside a bain-marie or dish of hot water, which prevents the pudding from cooking too fast. Steamed Pumpkin Pudding keeps for several days, covered, in the refrigerator, but loses the desired texture if frozen.

> *Safflower oil, for greasing pan*
> 1 *cup cooked pumpkin purée (canned)*
> 1 *teaspoon melted butter*
> ⅔ *cup buttermilk*
> 2 *eggs, lightly beaten*
> 2 *egg whites, lightly beaten*
> ¼ *cup maple syrup*
> ½ *teaspoon grated fresh ginger*
> 1½ *cups whole wheat pastry flour*
> ¼ *cup date sugar (ground, dried dates)*
> 2 *teaspoons baking soda*
> 2 *teaspoons cinnamon*
> 1 *teaspoon nutmeg*

1. Preheat oven to 375° F. Lightly oil a 1½-quart bundt or cake pan. Fill a larger pan ¼ full with hot water.

2. In a bowl combine pumpkin purée, butter, buttermilk, eggs, egg whites, maple syrup, and ginger. In a separate bowl sift together flour, date sugar, baking soda, cinnamon, and nutmeg.

3. Combine contents of both bowls and spoon into prepared bundt pan. Place pan into pan of hot water. Carefully set on middle oven rack and bake until a knife inserted in the center of the pudding comes out clean (30 to 40 minutes). Let cool 10 minutes before serving.

Serves 8.

> *Calories per serving: 178*
> *Preparation time: 20 minutes*
> *Baking time: 30–40 minutes*

TOFU-STRAWBERRY MOUSSE

Tofu (the Japanese name for bean curd) is a highly nutritious product made from soybeans that has been made in east Asia for over 2,000 years and is an important source of protein for millions of people. As both Asian foods and vegetarian diets grow in popularity in this country, tofu, available in many forms, is becoming a common supermarket item that you should have no trouble finding.

This very low-calorie dessert will surprise your guests—no one will believe it contains tofu. Be sure to buy soft tofu for this recipe; the firmer type tends to impart a grainier texture to the mousse. Also make sure that the tofu is extremely fresh because it will turn bitter as it ages. For a special garnish, make small parallel cuts in the tops of strawberries and press lightly to fan. You can make the mousse up to two hours before serving.

> ¼ *pound soft tofu, drained*
> 2 *cups strawberries, fresh or frozen, plus sliced strawberries for garnish*
> 2 *small ripe bananas*
> ½ *teaspoon nutmeg*
> 2 *teaspoons maple syrup*
> *Mint leaves, for garnish*

In a blender or food processor, combine all ingredients except the garnishes, puréeing thoroughly. Spoon into wineglasses, garnish, and chill for 30 minutes before serving.

Serves 4.

> *Calories per serving: 104*
> *Preparation time: 15 minutes*
> *Chilling time: 30 minutes*

LOW-CALORIE ICED DESSERTS

These easy-to-prepare iced desserts are great for snacks or impromptu entertaining on hot summer evenings, and kids love them. For creamier ices, freeze the mixture to the slush point, then blend and re-freeze in paper cups or swirled into wineglasses.

Orange Swirl Purée 2 cups fresh, peeled oranges with 1 tablespoon maple syrup and 1 teaspoon lemon juice. Freeze the purée in scooped-out orange halves.

Strawberry Pops Purée 2 cups fresh strawberries with 1 tablespoon apple juice concentrate. Freeze in small paper cups and when half frozen insert a wooden ice cream stick in the center. When frozen, peel away the cup.

Grape Nuggets Wash 2 cups seedless green or red grapes. Place on a baking sheet and freeze whole. Eat while still frozen.

A delicate apple strudel, fresh apple tart with a filo pie crust, and light lemon cheesecake are fine low-calorie choices for special occasions (see pages 122–123).

TARTS, CAKES, AND PIES

These delectable pastries cut the calories of regular pastry in half by using filo dough instead of butter-laden pie crusts; lightening the sweetener by relying on the natural sweetness of fresh fruits; and substituting blended skim-milk cheeses for pastry creams. So go ahead and indulge!

LEMON DREAM CHEESECAKE

Cheescake is a treat that many weight-conscious people ignore altogether, thinking that it is too extravagant for any diet. Not so for this recipe. This crustless cheesecake, which looks like a custard, sits inside a springform pan and uses nonfat yogurt and whipped Neufchâtel cheese—a lower-calorie but still-rich version of the real thing. Make Lemon Dream Cheesecake the day before and serve it to delighted guests at tea.

  ½ teaspoon safflower oil, for
    greasing pan
    Grated rind of 2 lemons
  ⅔ cup lemon juice
  1 envelope unflavored gelatin
  ½ cup Neufchâtel cheese
  ½ cup part-skim ricotta cheese
  1 cup plain, nonfat yogurt
  ¼ cup maple syrup
  3 egg whites

1. Lightly oil a springform pan. In a small saucepan place lemon rind, juice, and gelatin. Let stand 5 minutes, then heat until gelatin dissolves.

2. In a blender purée Neufchâtel, ricotta, yogurt, and maple syrup together until smooth. Combine with lemon mixture.

3. Beat egg whites until stiff peaks form. Fold into cheese mixture and spoon into prepared springform pan.

4. Chill the cheesecake for 4 hours or overnight. Serve chilled.

Serves 8 to 10.

> *Calories per serving: 94*
> *Preparation time: 20 minutes*
> *Chilling time: 4 hours*

FILO TART WITH RASPBERRIES

Made from flour, cornstarch, and water, filo is a delicate, paper-thin pastry. Directions for using filo dough are on page 123, and this recipe uses the same procedure: lightly dotting the filo with melted butter and layering the dough in a tart or pie pan to form a crust. Kiwifruit, mandarin orange slices, ripe peach, or any other soft fruit will work well if raspberries are unavailable.

    Safflower oil, for greasing
      tart pan
  4 sheets filo dough
  1½ tablespoons melted butter
  1 cup part-skim ricotta cheese
  1 teaspoon maple syrup
  1 teaspoon grated lemon rind
  1 teaspoon honey
  2 cups raspberries

1. Preheat oven to 375° F. Lightly oil a 9½-inch tart pan.

2. Lightly brush the top surface of a filo sheet with butter. Fit into the prepared tart pan, building up the sides to make edges. Repeat with remaining sheets of filo dough. With scissors, trim the filo dough extending beyond the edge of the tart shell. Line filo dough with aluminum foil and fill the foil with dried beans. Bake the tart shell until golden (about 20 minutes). Let cool.

3. In a blender purée ricotta, maple syrup, and lemon rind.

4. Brush the baked, cooled tart shell with ½ teaspoon of the honey. Spoon the ricotta mixture into the shell and layer the berries on top. Brush tops of berries with remaining honey. Serve chilled or at room temperature.

Serves 8.

> *Calories per serving: 115*
> *Preparation time: 20 minutes*
> *Baking time: 20 minutes*

APPLE STRUDEL

In this easy recipe sheets of buttered filo dough are wrapped around a simple apple filling into a log shape, and baked. You can make this strudel with almost any kind of fruit filling: cranberries, sliced pears, peaches, or rhubarb.

  3 cups sliced tart apples, such as
    Granny Smith or McIntosh
  ½ cup apple juice
  2 tablespoons arrowroot powder
  ¼ cup maple syrup
  1 teaspoon cinnamon
  ¼ cup raisins
  ¼ cup chopped, pitted fresh dates
    Oil, for greasing baking sheet
  4 sheets filo dough
  1½ tablespoons melted butter
  1 teaspoon chopped almonds

1. In a heavy saucepan place apples and apple juice, cover, and cook for 3 minutes at high heat to soften. Meanwhile, blend together arrowroot, maple syrup, cinnamon, raisins, and dates.

2. Preheat oven to 400° F. Lightly oil an aluminum-foil–lined baking sheet.

3. Brush 1 sheet of filo dough with butter and lay it on the lined baking sheet. Repeat with second sheet, placing it on top of the first. Continue with remaining 2 sheets, saving a small amount of the butter for top of strudel.

4. Mix apples and arrowroot mixture. Spoon along one of the short edges of the stack of dough; fold in the 2 longer edges to create sides that will prevent liquid from running out as you roll.

5. Roll strudel into a log, sealing in the filling. Place seam side down on lined baking sheet. Brush top with a small amount of butter and dust with almonds.

6. Bake until lightly browned (about 30 minutes). Let cool, then cut into 8 slices.

Serves 8.

> *Calories per serving: 153*
> *Preparation time: 25 minutes*
> *Baking time: 30 minutes*

SWEET POTATO CREAM PIE

A low-calorie variation of a traditional southern sweet potato pie, this recipe uses brown-rice cereal, or rice cream, as a thickener. You can make your own rice cream by simply blending uncooked brown rice in a blender until powdery. The crust of this pie is made from crushed whole wheat graham crackers, which are available in health-food stores. With its warm color and harvest-time appeal, Sweet Potato Cream Pie makes an ideal Thanksgiving dinner dessert.

Safflower oil, for greasing
2 *cups crushed whole wheat, unsweetened graham crackers*
1½ *cups apple juice, or as needed to moisten graham crackers*
2 *large sweet potatoes*
1 *cup brown-rice cream cereal*
2 *teaspoons unroasted sesame tahini*
2 *tablespoons light honey*
⅓ *cup apple juice*
1 *teaspoon allspice*
2 *teaspoons grated fresh ginger*
¼ *teaspoon cloves*

1. Preheat oven to 375° F. Lightly oil a 9-inch pie plate.

2. Mix thoroughly crushed graham crackers with apple juice; carefully press mixture onto bottom and sides of prepared pie plate. Set aside.

3. Steam sweet potatoes until very soft (about 30 minutes).

4. In a blender or food processor blend sweet potatoes with remaining ingredients until mixture is smooth and creamy. Pour into pie shell.

5. Bake until firm (30 to 40 minutes). Let cool before slicing.

Serves 8 to 10.

Calories per serving: 179
Preparation time: 75 minutes
Baking time: 40 minutes

APPLE TART

Apple tart looks and tastes like the traditional French apple pastries seen in patisseries, but this has half the calories. Apple Tart uses a filo crust (see at right) and a light honey glaze. Choose tart apples, such as Granny Smith or Winesap for best flavor.

Safflower oil, for greasing
4 *sheets filo dough*
1½ *tablespoons melted butter*
4 *cups peeled, cored, and thinly sliced tart apples*
1 *teaspoon honey*
¾ *cup unsweetened applesauce*

1. Preheat oven to 375° F. Lightly oil a 9½-inch pie plate or tart tin.

2. Lightly brush top surface of a filo sheet with butter. Fit into prepared pie plate, building up sides to make edges. Repeat procedure with the next sheet, continuing to stack the remaining buttered sheets in the plate. With scissors, trim excess off edge of tart shell. Line shell with aluminum foil and fill with dried beans. Bake tart shell until golden (about 20 minutes). Let cool.

3. Place sliced apples on a lightly oiled baking sheet. Sprinkle with water. Bake for 10 minutes in a 375° F oven. Remove and let cool 10 minutes.

4. Brush the baked, cooled tart shell with half the honey. Spread applesauce over the filo. With a metal spatula or knife, gently place the cooked apple slices in a fan pattern around the top of the applesauce. Brush with remaining honey. Serve warm for best flavor.

Serves 8.

Calories per serving: 102
Preparation time: 20 minutes
Baking time: 20 minutes

Basics

HOW TO WORK WITH FILO DOUGH

Filo dough is fragile pastry made from flour, cornstarch, and water. It is rolled so thin that you can see the silhouette of your hand through it.

If you buy filo dough frozen, make sure it thaws completely before you use it. As you peel off the layers of dough, the edges will tend to stick if moisture remains from the freezing process.

Keep filo dough wrapped until ready to use. Some chefs cover the filo with a slightly dampened towel or a piece of plastic wrap. Make sure your work surface is clean and dry.

You must brush each layer of filo dough with melted butter before baking, so that it will puff up. Usually ¼ to ½ cup of butter is used per pound of filo. For low-calorie filo pastries, use very little melted butter by lightly sprinkling it on the pastry, then spreading it with a pastry brush.

Once filo pastries are buttered, filled, and ready to cook, they can be wrapped in plastic and stored for up to 2 days in the refrigerator. It is best to cook filo in a very hot (400° to 425° F) oven, so that the butter expands quickly and the filo puffs well.

INDEX

Note: Page numbers in italics refer to photographs separated from recipe text.

U.S. MEASURE AND METRIC MEASURE CONVERSION CHART

		Formulas for Exact Measures			Rounded Measures for Quick Reference		
	Symbol	When you know:	Multiply by:	To find:			
Mass (Weight)	oz	ounces	28.35	grams	1 oz		= 30 g
	lb	pounds	0.45	kilograms	4 oz		= 115 g
	g	grams	0.035	ounces	8 oz		= 225 g
	kg	kilograms	2.2	pounds	16 oz	= 1 lb	= 450 g
					32 oz	= 2 lb	= 900 g
					36 oz	= 2¼ lb	= 1,000g (1 kg)
Volume	tsp	teaspoons	5.0	milliliters	¼ tsp	= ¹⁄₂₄ oz	= 1 ml
	tbsp	tablespoons	15.0	milliliters	½ tsp	= ¹⁄₁₂ oz	= 2 ml
	fl oz	fluid ounces	29.57	milliliters	1 tsp	= ⅙ oz	= 5 ml
	c	cups	0.24	liters	1 tbsp	= ½ oz	= 15 ml
	pt	pints	0.47	liters	1 c	= 8 oz	= 250 ml
	qt	quarts	0.95	liters	2 c (1 pt)	= 16 oz	= 500 ml
	gal	gallons	3.785	liters	4 c (1 qt)	= 32 oz	= 1 liter
	ml	milliliters	0.034	fluid ounces	4 qt (1 gal)	= 128 oz	= 3¾ liter
Length	in.	inches	2.54	centimeters	⅜ in.		= 1 cm
	ft	feet	30.48	centimeters	1 in.		= 2.5 cm
	yd	yards	0.9144	meters	2 in.		= 5 cm
	mi	miles	1.609	kilometers	2½ in.		= 6.5 cm
	km	kilometers	0.621	miles	12 in. (1 ft)		= 30 cm
	m	meters	1.094	yards	1 yd		= 90 cm
	cm	centimeters	0.39	inches	100 ft		= 30 m
					1 mi		= 1.6 km
Temperature	°F	Fahrenheit	⁵⁄₉ (after subtracting 32)	Celsius	32°F		= 0°C
					68°F		= 20°C
	°C	Celsius	⁹⁄₅ (then add 32)	Fahrenheit	212°F		= 100°C
Area	in.²	square inches	6.452	square centimeters	1 in.²		= 6.5 cm²
	ft²	square feet	929.0	square centimeters	1 ft²		= 930 cm²
	yd²	square yards	8361.0	square centimeters	1 yd²		= 8360 cm²
	a.	acres	0.4047	hectares	1 a.		= 4050 m²